D0645870

COULD YOU EVER COME BACK
TO THE CATHOLIC CHURCH?

Could You Ever Come Back to the Catholic Church?

LORENE HANLEY DUQUIN

Afterword by Henry J. Mansell, D.D.
Bishop of Buffalo

ST PAULS

Library of Congress Cataloging-in-Publication Data

Duquin, Lorene Hanley.
    Could you ever come back to the Catholic Church? / Lorene Hanley
  Duquin.
        p.   cm.
    ISBN 0-8189-0789-4
    1. Ex-church members — Catholic Church. 2. Catholic Church —
  Doctrines.   I. Title.
  BX2347.8.E82D86   1997
  282 — dc21   96-40145
                                                              CIP

Produced and designed in the United States of America by the
Fathers and Brothers of the Society of St. Paul,
2187 Victory Boulevard, Staten Island, New York 10314-6603,
as part of their communications apostolate.

ISBN: 0-8189-0789-4

Printing Information:

Current Printing - first digit   3   4   5   6   7   8   9   10

Year of Current Printing - first year shown

               2004 2005 2006 2007 2008 2009 2010 2011 2012

To Dick,
whose decision to become Catholic
brought hundreds of people back
to the Church — including me!

Table of Contents

Acknowledgments

This book would not have been possible without the help of nearly one hundred people who shared their stories in personal interviews or through e-mail on the Internet.

I am deeply indebted to Father John Catoir, whose concern for unchurched and alienated Catholics has led to the start of St. Jude Media Ministry, which broadcasts radio messages of hope to people who have drifted away from God or the practice of their faith.

Father Flavian Walsh, OFM, of the Holy Name Province, provided a wealth of information and insights from his experiences with the Come Home program in New York City. I am also indebted to Father Ronald Pecci, OFM, also of the Holy Name Province, who brought the Come Home program to upstate New York and offered valuable insights on the programs and the people.

Two of my favorite Jesuits offered their expert advice: Father James Hennesey, SJ, of LeMoyne College in Syracuse helped with the historical sections, and Father James Lee Dugan, SJ, of Canisius College in Buffalo helped with psychological issues.

Without the help of Father Robert Kennedy of the St. Bernard Institute in Rochester, New York, and Father Jac Campbell, CSP, Joan Horn, and Mariann Ferretti of Landings, I would still be struggling to understand some of the differences between the various programs for alienated Catholics that are available nationwide.

Sister Margaret Krantz, FMDC, of Williamsville, New York was an invaluable resource for bereavement issues.

To Father Bob Hughes of Westmont, New Jersey and Father Paul Bombadier of Ware, Massachusetts, a special thank you for the e-mail interviews.

Special thanks also go to Jean Fox and Father Emile Briere of Madonna House in Combermere, Ontario.

Most of all, however, I am grateful to Bishop Henry Mansell for writing the Afterword, and to the following priests from the Diocese of Buffalo, who shared their experiences and insights in their personal ministries and in the "Come Home" program: Father Gary J. Bagley, Msgr. Vincent J. Becker, Father Leon J. Biernat, Msgr. Angelo M. Caligiuri, Father Thomas D. Doyle, Msgr. William J. Gallagher, Father David G. LiPuma, Father Paul M. Nogaro, Father Joseph S. Rogliano, Msgr. William G. Stanton, Msgr. Rupert A. Wright, Father Dan Young, Father Richard E. Zajac, and Father Robert E. Zapfel.

COULD YOU EVER COME BACK
TO THE CATHOLIC CHURCH?

CHAPTER 1

Could You Ever Come Back to the Catholic Church?

"I have not been a member of the Church for many years. I now miss the feeling of peace that it gave me. I would appreciate any advice on finding my way home again." *Laura Humes, Stevensville, Michigan*

"Let's just say that before I left the Church (or was booted — I'm not sure which!) I spent much of my time on religious pursuits. It was very important to me and I miss those days sometimes. But I don't know about going back." *C. Bruce Santore II, Reynoldsburg, Ohio*

"I was raised Catholic. I was married by a priest and a minister in a joint ceremony, but afterward I joined the Presbyterian Church. Now I'm getting a divorce and want to consider rejoining the Catholic Church. What are my options? Will I be restricted because of the divorce?" *R.B., Santa Cruz, California*

"I am still struggling with my faith and have a lot of guilt for not being a good Catholic. My son asked me the other day why we don't go to church anymore. I didn't know what to tell him. I need to get past all the bad experiences I've had. I need to think about what is really important to me and try to remember how I felt before those bad experiences. I wish there were more programs or support

1

groups in my area for people like me going through a struggle." *E.C., Kentucky*

The decision whether or not to come back to the Catholic Church almost always involves a struggle.

"The way it looked in my head before I returned to the Catholic Church was this big, scary 'RETURNING' as if I'd walk in on a Sunday and some sort of scarlet letter ("R" for Returning, or maybe "D" for Deserter!) would appear on me. Then everyone would turn and look at me and imagine what awful things I'd been doing during those years of non-attendance. Okay, it's a little dramatic, but I actually did have nightmares about going back." *Janice Haber, Guthrie, Oklahoma*

Some people say it feels as if they are suspended in mid-air with cosmic forces drawing them in opposite directions. On one side they feel a powerful attraction, almost like the pull of a magnet, that draws them gently and yet persistently toward a sense of peace, love, and purpose.

"Every day on my way to school I passed a church that I had attended twenty years ago. When I passed this church I felt a strong pull towards it. I wanted to go in." *Carol Samuelson, Jamestown, New York*

At the same time, another part of them reels in horror: "ARE YOU CRAZY??!! THIS IS THE CATHOLIC CHURCH. NOTHING HAS CHANGED. YOU CAN'T GO BACK. YOU'LL ONLY FIND MORE PAIN, MORE DISILLUSIONMENT, MORE REJECTION."

"I am afraid to walk into a church. As much as these thoughts are irrational, I am afraid to go back." *S.N., Ridgewood, New Jersey*

At various stages, people feel angry, defensive, remorseful, defiant, hopeless and helpless. Yet from the moment they acknowledge that gentle pull, they can't ignore it. If you're reading this book because you've felt that same inner struggle, you might be interested in knowing that there are millions of others in the same situation.

- Between 15 and 20 million Catholics in the United States are away from the Church.

- A recent Gallup poll reported that 40% of alienated Catholics said they would come back to the Church if they felt the Church wanted them, which means up to 8 million people feel some sort of longing to come home.

In some parts of the country, particularly in large metropolitan areas, dioceses and parishes run special programs or information sessions specifically designed to invite lapsed Catholics back without any pressure or commitment. The structure of these programs may vary, but whether the program is called "Come Home," or "Re-Membering," or "Landings," or "Another Look," or "Alienated Catholics Anonymous" the goal is always the same: To provide a warm, non-judgmental environment where people can explore without pressure the reasons they left the Church and whether or not they want to return.

Unfortunately, in too many parts of the country there are no safe, anonymous sessions where a lapsed Catholic can ask questions, get answers, and find the help they need. The purpose of this book is to recreate on paper the experience of a typical "Come Home" session. The stories, questions, and concerns are all taken from real life people. Since some of them have chosen anonymity, details may be changed slightly to assure privacy. Each story is unique, just as your story is unique. You may, however, recognize your questions in their questions, your struggles in their struggles, and your pain in their feelings of anger, rejection, guilt, fear, confusion, doubt, sadness, and separation. No matter what emotions a fallen-away Catholic experiences, beneath the surface the common denominator is pain. In the process of coming home, many people find that they have to slice open old wounds and let the poison of the past drain out before they can be healed. How deeply you delve into your own story is entirely up to you. Ultimately, it's your decision. Some choose to return:

> "I came back to the Sacraments after a 15-year absence and it felt like my wedding day, only more profound! I could not stop crying." G.L.

Others stay away:

> "So far, I have not returned to any church. I think the Church has finally pushed me away for good."
> K.M., Wichita, Kansas

Some postpone the decision and do nothing for a while:

> "My actual return to confession and full participation in a parish took about three years after I felt the first longing."
> T.D.

No matter what you decide, the only commitment you should make is to be open and honest. The next step is identifying the reasons you feel separated from the Church. J.P. Morgan once said, "There are two reasons why a man does anything. There's the good reason, and there's the *real* reason." You can probably rattle off several good reasons for leaving the Church. Uncovering the real reason may require a little more soul-searching.

Most people discover that coming back to the Church is not an event as much as it is a process that involves a little pain, a little laughter, some thinking, some prayer, some discernment and a lot of letting go. You may begin to feel like Dorothy in

The Wizard of Oz searching for a way to come home and not knowing that the ability to find what you are looking for is within you. Like Dorothy, in order to really believe that you can come home, you may have to follow the yellow brick road through darkness and light, through scary forests and beautiful fields, meeting friends and enemies along the way, yet feeling strangely alone. You'll know you are home when you begin to feel a deep sense of peace.

CHAPTER 2

Why Did You Leave?

"I remarried outside the Church, and there's no hope of ever getting an annulment. I don't expect that the Catholic Church will ever actively seek reconciliation with those of us who are divorced and remarried." *E.G.*

"I left the Catholic Church in 1968 at age 16 because I was both searching for the truth and being seduced by the counter culture of the 60's. Four years later, I had a dramatic encounter with the Holy Spirit and since that time I have been fellowshipping in evangelical and moderate Charismatic circles." *Angelo Natalie, Connecticut*

"I became irritated at Mass by what seemed like a continual barrage of preaching against abortion, not only during the homily but at every possible opportunity. After a prolonged absence, I stopped in for Stations of the Cross during Lent, and at every Station Father's remarks contrived to reveal another evil facet of abortion. I do not believe in abortion, but I don't feel comfortable at all about badgering, bothering, and otherwise harassing those who do. Perhaps I just find it too difficult to treat a pulpit like a soapbox." *M.R.*

"I was in fourth grade when my dad died. He was a diabetic alcoholic. I remember many nights when I would pray that my dad would quit drinking. When he passed away, I remember thinking that I spent all this time praying to God and my prayers were not answered. By age 14, I fell away from the Church." *Joe MacKay, Seattle, Washington*

There are as many reasons for leaving the Catholic Church as there are people who leave. In a 1980 study, David A. Roozen found that 42% of all Catholics drop out during some time in their lives. Other researchers have tried to categorize the reasons why.

Dean R. Hoge, in a study for the United States Catholic Conference, identified interfaith marriage as the greatest single reason people leave the Catholic Church, but he also noted that interfaith marriage is the greatest single source of new converts to Catholicism. Beyond the interfaith factor, Hoge compiled five broad categories of Catholics who drop out for other reasons:

1. **Family Tension Dropouts**: These people grew up with tensions in their families, and as soon as they were old enough, they rebelled against both the family and the Church.

2. **Weary Dropouts**: These people felt bored by the Church and stopped going when pressure from parents or a spouse ended, or when their children grew up and there was no longer a need to set a role model for them.

3. **Lifestyle Dropouts**: These people's lives do not comply with Church laws. They include people who are divorced and remarried, those in homosexual relationships, unmarried couples living together, etc.

4. **Spiritual Need Dropouts**: These people find that their spiritual needs are not met by the Catholic Church. Some simply stay away. Others are attracted to non-Catholic churches for worship, prayer, Bible study, and a sense of community.

5. **Anti-change Dropouts**: These people objected to changes in the Church after Vatican II. They prefer the Latin Mass and feel uneasy with liturgical innovations and changes in Church laws.

The late Father Alvin A. Illig, CSP, who formed a ministry to alienated Catholics in conjunction with the Paulist National Catholic Evangelization Association, agreed that marriage to a non-Catholic poses the greatest threat to a person's Catholicism, but he added a few more categories to the list:

- People turned off by ineffective preaching of the word of God.

- Families who fail to join a parish within the first six months of a move to a different location.

- People who feel there has not been enough change in the Church in matters relating to birth control, women's ordination, divorce, intercommunion with other faiths.

- A personal quarrel, abuse, or rejection by a priest or parish staff member.

- Deterioration of Catholic family life and religious practices in the home.

- Diminishing loyalty to a parish and the tendency to attend Mass at different parishes without affiliating.

- Confusion over the teaching authority of the Church and what Catholics believe.

- The impersonal nature of large suburban parishes with fewer priests.

- The impact of secular and materialistic influences in society that draws people away from a religious or spiritual consciousness.

In a 1985 Gallup Poll commissioned by Father Illig, lapsed Catholics cited the following reasons for leaving:

- Lack of interest in the Catholic Church or religion in general.

- Inability to accept certain Church teachings.

- Divorce.

- Feeling that the Church was drifting too far from the Bible.

- Objections to what they saw as Church emphasis on money.

Statistics also show that 40% of Catholics between the ages of 15 and 29 leave the Church for at least two years.

"If young people wander away, it's usually after Confirmation or high school," says Father Joe Rogliano of Amherst, New York, who meets hundreds of lapsed teens and young adults. "They usually come back. It might be through marriage. It might be through a baptism or a funeral. They might run into someone from their old parish. I've met lots of people who will take issue with certain things about the Church. Sometimes through that conversation they might call or come around. Others stay away because they just don't want to deal with it. Sometimes they're not ready to look inside and see if it has to do with their own need for a personal reconciliation."

Father Flavian Walsh, OFM, one of the founders of the Come Home Program at St. Francis Church in New York City, agrees that in most cases fallen-away teens and college students don't have a serious problem. "That's not losing your faith," he says. "They are young Catholics who are on vacation for a while."

Father Flavian has compiled his own reasons why people leave the Church, and topping his list are divorced and remarried Catholics. "That's the biggest group," he says. "Birth control used to be an issue but not as much today."

He lists other key reasons as:

- fear of confession

- ignorance of basic catechesis

- guilt
- boring, irrelevant homilies
- bad experience at the hands of a cleric or religious
- the political and social standings of the Church
- women's issues
- gay and lesbian issues

Father Flavian is quick to note, however, that underlying these reasons there are often deeper wounds that someone who has been away from the Church may or may not want to address. After three years in the Come Home program, he did an informal survey of 800 participants and discovered that many alienated Catholics also struggle with:

- a deep sense of failure, such as the feeling that they have failed God, their parents, their children, or their friends.
- a destroyed or damaged self-image, fear of intimacy or the inability to love.
- pain that never went away after the loss of a loved one through death or divorce.
- a sense of hopelessness, meaninglessness or despair.
- the inability to integrate human sexuality into life.
- chronic alcoholism or drug addiction in the person or a family member.
- hidden guilt over some action or event that has been masked over for years.
- marital misery, lack of communication and loneliness.
- disillusionment with short-term relationships or abuse of sexual freedom.
- fear of death, hell or eternal damnation.

Father Flavian creates a separate category for people who

are angry at the Church. One woman told him she wanted to be president of POC's.

"What's that?" he asked.

"Pissed off Catholics," she fumed.

This woman had worked hard to put her husband through professional school. After he got established in his career, he divorced her, got an annulment, and married his secretary. "She wanted to nail the Catholic Church to a wall for granting that annulment," Father Flavian recalled. "You don't get over hurts this deep in one or two sessions."

In the booklet *Penance: A Reform Proposal for the Rite*, Father James Lopresti proposed that all of the reasons people leave can be consolidated into three categories:

- **The Unawakened**: These people may have been raised in the Catholic Church, but never developed a personal, adult relationship with Jesus Christ and the Church.

- **The Prophetically Alienated**: These people claim, rightly or wrongly, that the Church has compromised the Gospel message.

- **The Truly Alienated**: These people know the Gospel message but have chosen to reject it.

Chances are you can probably relate to one or more of these reasons. You might even have a few reasons of your own to add. It's a good idea to make a list. Then rank your reasons in order of their importance. Ask yourself: Which ones are the *good* reasons and which ones are the *real* reasons?

"One thing that jumps out at me is that people who have a strong aversion to Catholicism are often not as concerned about questions of faith as they are about questions of behavior." *S.L., New Jersey*

Frank Johnston of Cumming, Georgia agrees:

"By the time I started college, I decided 'agnostic' was a good description for me. After college, I joined the Air Force. My dog tags read: 'No Religious Preference.'

"To sum it up, I couldn't profess to believe in God because that would have required an evaluation of my behavior and I wasn't looking to change my behavior."

As you go through the reasons why you feel separated from the Church, make a note of what feelings arise with each entry. "I once thought feelings were like sneezes," writes Father John Powell, a Jesuit psychologist. "They come and go harmlessly. They are really not very important. Now I think that feelings are critically important... and they are diagnostic of what is really in us."

As Father Powell suggests, the emotions that arise might give you a clue as to what really matters in the deepest part of your being.

"If I'm given the opportunity, I always try to get down to the wound," says Father Joe Rogliano. "I try to cut through all the arguments and the positioning, and ask, 'What is really going on?' I go to where the sore spot is, uncover it, and find out what's really festering down there."

"I think many people felt pressured to leave the Church because of external forces," says Father Paul Nogaro of Kenmore, New York, who has worked with hundreds of alienated Catholics. "There are some people who make an intellectual commitment to leave, but for other people it is not a well thought out thing, and these people might be interested in giving it another try. There's a certain pull that Catholicism has on people. You can't shrug it off that easily. I don't think that most people who leave make a total break so there's always a link or some residue."

Chapter Notes

42% of all Catholics drop out...: David A. Roozen, "Church Dropouts: Changing Patterns of Disengagement and Re-entry," *Review of Religious Research*, 21:427-50, 1980.

In a 1981 study: Dean R. Hoge, *Converts, Dropouts, Returnees: A Study of Religious Change Among Catholics*, United States Catholic Conference, New York: The Pilgrim Press, 1981.

A 1985 Gallup Poll...: George J. Gallup and Jim Castelli, *The American Catholic People, Their Beliefs, Practices and Values*, New York, Doubleday & Company, 1987.

In the booklet *Penance: A Reform Proposal for the Rite*...: Sarah Harmony, *Re-Membering, The Ministry of Welcoming Alienated and Inactive Catholics*, Collegeville, Minnesota: The Liturgical Press, 1991, pp. 14-16.

"I once thought feelings...": John Powell, *Solving the Riddle of Self: The Search for Self-Discovery*, Allen, Texas: Thomas More, a Division of Tabor Publishing, 1995, pp. 61-62.

CHAPTER 3

What Would You Need?

"I used to think I knew what being a Catholic was; however, after over 25 years of Catholic education and undergoing John XXIII reformation of our worshipping structure, I seem confused over what a Catholic is." *N.D.*

"I'm twice divorced and currently married outside the Church. I've been away for some 30 years and my yearning has been to return, but I don't know the way through all the divorces, annulments, excommunications, etc." *H.R.M., California*

"I liked the traditions and 'pageantry' of the Church, but there are just too many of the Church teachings that I can't accept like the bans on birth control, female priests, married priests, etc. Can I hold onto my own beliefs and still become a Catholic?" *S.K.*

One of the main advantages of a "Come Home" program is that people can openly discuss their questions, concerns and needs. Often, participants provide support and encouragement for each other.

Tim Denesha discovered this phenomenon at a Come Home session in upstate New York where nearly 200 people had gathered in a Catholic school gymnasium. Tim felt especially nervous when he found himself seated in a small discussion group with people who were all divorced and remarried outside the Church.

"Why are you here?" asked a man, who looked and sounded like Archie Bunker.

Tim took a deep breath. "I'm gay, and the Church has been very intolerant and unjust to gay people."

"See!" Archie Bunker shot back. "The Church shafted you, too!"

Then someone else chimed in, "Maybe you can find a parish where the pastor is enlightened about gays."

Was I hallucinating, Tim wondered, *or were straight Catholics helping to reconcile me to the Church which had also hurt them?*

After a while, each group reported their concerns, which were written on a large blackboard.

Tim's group hadn't discussed which of their comments to share, but when their turn came, Archie Bunker stood and loudly proclaimed, "I need to feel accepted and respected as a gay man on equal terms with other Catholics, not as a second class citizen."

"This straight guy had read my need verbatim, as if it were his own!" Tim recalled. "As we broke up, I thanked him for voicing my need."

"Well," he shrugged, "all we kept hearing about was divorce, birth control and sexism. I figured you probably weren't the only gay person here."

Tim Denesha was not the only nervous person, either. On the first night of any Come Home session, the mood is always tense. People sit with arms folded. There are no cheerful expressions. Sometimes the anger in the room is almost palpable.

Father Dan Young had been ordained less than a year when he joined a Come Home team in Buffalo, New York. "Nothing I learned in the seminary prepared me for that kind of anger," this 28-year-old priest recalled. "These people were angry and they were lashing out at me. I had to think to myself: *They aren't personally lashing out at me. Some of them are angry about things that happened before I was even born! But I repre-*

sent something to them. I represent the Catholic Church. It was tough, but it was very good for me. I had to find ways to deal with this anger. I kept thinking: *If Jesus Christ were here, what would he do?* I found myself apologizing for any priest or religious that might have hurt these people in the past. That broke the tension."

Sometimes the tension breaks when a facilitator is able to make the group laugh. Father Flavian Walsh recalls the first Come Home session in New York City:

> One woman had been away from the Church for over 20 years. She was dressed to kill and sat in the second row, first seat. There were 40 or 50 people. No one was smiling.
>
> I said, "Does anyone want to break the ice? What did the Church do to hurt you?"
>
> This woman stood up and said, "You screwed up my sex life."
>
> I turned to the blackboard and wrote: "Screwed up sex life."
>
> "What year was it?" I asked.
>
> "1962," she replied.
>
> "Whew!" I said. "I was in Japan. It wasn't me!"
>
> She laughed and then everyone else in the room started to laugh. As it turns out, this woman was a graduate of some Catholic women's college where the teachings about sexuality were so negative that she never married. She blamed the Church for that.

Sometimes, a Come Home group can get so focused on the sexual teachings of the Church that they lose perspective. When that happens, Father Flavian goes to the blackboard and with a very serious face, he writes S-E-X.

> Then I turn around and say, "We'll get back to this eventually, but for the next hour and a half, there are to be no questions about that area of life."

The room becomes dead silent, but then somebody giggles. The giggle catches on, and more people start giggling. Then someone will say, "Well, what are we going to talk about?" And the whole room bursts into laughter.

That's my opening. I go to the blackboard and I say, "What about faith, hope, love, compassion, peace, joy, forgiveness, justice? There's more in the Gospels about these things than there is about sex. If we can stop being a morality religion and start being a faith religion, we'll get back to where the Gospel wants us to be. Most of the questions on sex are solved when you delve into these other areas. We act what we believe. If you can develop these other areas, the area of sex will take care of itself."

What are the areas of concern that you would need addressed before making a decision to come back to the Church? Take a few moments and jot them down. Then compare your list with the following needs, questions and concerns expressed at Come Home programs over the years:

• Are you still Catholic if you believe but don't go to church?

• Can you give me information on Confirmation and First Communion for people who have been away?

• Where do divorced and remarried people stand with the Church?

• What do I have to do to get an annulment?

• What steps does someone have to take to come back to the Church?

• Are gays and lesbians accepted in the Church?

• What is the Church stand on gay priests?

• What are the conditions for receiving Communion? Who can and cannot receive the Eucharist?

- Can people who are divorced receive the Sacraments? What about divorced and remarried people?

- Can you give us information on how to go to Confession?

- How did Confession change after Vatican II? Do you have to go face-to-face?

- I am concerned about politics in the Church.

- Will women ever be ordained?

- Can you receive the Sacraments if you were married in a civil ceremony?

- Can someone offer some kind of help for interfaith marriages? What is more important: Family unity with everyone going to a Protestant Church or should the Catholic member of the family separate from the rest and attend Mass alone?

- If I come back to the Church what would I have to do to bring my children back?

- Why should someone belong to the Church?

- I heard about something called Internal Forum for people in invalid marriages. What is it?

- Could someone explain the changes since Vatican II?

- How about an explanation of who makes Church rules, how they are made, and on what they are based.

- I'd like to explore the difference between God's rules, Church rules, and my rules. For instance, what do you do when your own personal beliefs on birth control or abortion differ with Church law?

- How do you cope with the loss of someone you love?

- Why does God allow bad things to happen?

- How can I overcome past hurts caused by priests and nuns?

- How can I forgive when it hurts so much?

- I question the hypocrisy in the Church, e.g., clergy and Church laws versus what happens in actual practice.
- Could you explain why there seems to be a double standard regarding the Sacraments, e.g., priests can commit terrible sins and still say Mass, but divorced and remarried Catholics are not allowed to receive Communion?
- I need to know how to pray.
- What if you are plagued with doubts about what you believe?
- What are the differences between venial and mortal sins?
- How do you deal with feelings of being rejected by the Church?
- How do you heal the painful memories associated with Catholicism and move on with your life?
- What happens to unbaptized people? My children have never been baptized.
- Where do fallen-away Catholics stand with God?

If you were at a Come Home program, all of these concerns would be examined during special sessions in the following weeks. The subsequent chapters of this book will attempt to recreate those special sessions on paper. Take what is useful. Ignore what is not. Seek help for areas that remain unclear or concerns left unaddressed. Keep an open mind, a listening heart, and pray for an increase in love, faith, courage, and understanding. Perhaps the best advice comes from the Austro-German poet and novelist Rainer Maria Rilke, who wrote:

> "Be patient toward all that is unsolved within you and try to love the questions themselves. The point is to live everything. Do not seek the answers that cannot be lived, but love the questions, and perhaps without knowing it you will live your way into the answers."

CHAPTER 4

Who Makes the Rules?

"I believe strongly in the Ten Commandments and the teachings of Jesus, but I disagree with 'rules' issued by the Catholic Church. I am not a sheep and do not follow the teachings of 'man' blindly." *C.S.*

"I think sometime in the future 'they' will change the rules again. At one time you absolutely could not eat meat on Friday, but now you can. If it was wrong then, but it's okay now, maybe the rules will change again in the future." *Rebecca Oliver, California*

"Are we following the Commandments of God or Rome?" *M.E., Pennsylvania*

Before the Second Vatican Council, most Catholics would never even think about questioning Church rules. People memorized the rules as children, and they knew exactly where they stood with God and the Church. Then, in the late 1960's, some of the rules changed. Things that used to be serious sins, like eating meat on Friday, disappeared from the rule book. In religion classes, children stopped memorizing catechisms and started singing songs. The emphasis shifted from following rules to taking personal responsibility for your relationship with God, the Church, and other people.

Today, there are still specific rules in the Catholic Church, but many Catholics seem less inclined to follow the letter of the law. When the Pope issues an official teaching on morality or social justice, news agencies conduct a poll to see what percentage of Catholics agree or disagree. The term "cafeteria Catholics" has emerged to describe people who pick and choose what rules they are going to follow. When asked in a recent survey about the statement: *Catholics should follow the teachings of the Pope and not take it upon themselves to decide differently*, only 25% agreed. In the same survey, only 9% of Catholics considered birth control wrong for married couples; about half (48%) considered pre-marital sex to be always wrong; 58% thought abortion is always wrong no matter what the circumstances; 61% thought priests should be allowed to marry; 42% favored women priests; and 52% supported capital punishment.

Some people see this as a crisis of authority in the Catholic Church, while others insist that it is not so much a crisis as it is confusion in the wake of a changing Church after Vatican II. Whether it is crisis or confusion, the issue almost always arises at Come Home sessions. People want to know:

• Who makes the rules?
• Who has the power to change the rules?
• What happens when one rule conflicts with another rule?
• What's the difference between God's rules, Church rules, and your own rules about right and wrong?

Essentially, the "rules" all come from God speaking through Scripture, through Tradition, through the laws of nature, through the Pope and the Bishops, and through your own conscience. For example, the Church teaches that some of God's "rules" come to us through Divine revelation in Scripture: "Thou shalt not kill... Thou shalt not steal... . Love God with all your heart... Love your neighbor as yourself."

The Church claims the authority to form laws based on how Divine revelation applies in society today. For example, the Church interprets "Thou shalt not kill..." as a prohibition against homicide, euthanasia, suicide, and abortion, with strong warnings that war and the death penalty are acceptable only in extreme cases. As new technologies develop, the Church tries to apply the teachings of the Gospel to ethical concerns such as the moral ramifications of organ transplants, do-not-resuscitate orders, physician assisted suicide, in-vitro fertilization, and genetic engineering.

If you agree with the teachings of the Church, there's no problem. Questions arise when Church laws conflict with what some people believe is right or wrong. "Who's the Pope?" they ask. "What right does the Church have to tell me what to do?"

When the Pope makes an official pronouncement, he cites "the authority which Christ conferred upon Peter and his Successors, and in communion with the Bishops of the Catholic Church." This authority comes from Matthew 16:17-18, in which Jesus establishes Peter as the first among the Apostles and says, "Whatever you bind on earth shall be bound in heaven; and whatever you loose on earth shall be loosed in heaven."

Catholics believe this authority has been passed on throughout the centuries. It is important to note, however, that Church teachings are never a question of how the Pope feels personally about an issue. The Pope and the bishops never originate new truths. Instead they guide the Church based on what has already been revealed.

When it comes to rules about the sacraments, liturgies, priestly duties, religious orders, and Church structure, you can find the answers in the Code of Canon Law, which contains 1752 specific laws that govern the inner workings of the Church. Canon law and the official teachings of the Church are universal and apply to all Catholics.

Bishops also have the authority to teach and govern in their own dioceses. For example, in March 1996, Bishop Michael D.

Pfeifer of San Angelo, Texas banned guns and weapons from all Church-owned property, but this rule is not binding on people in other dioceses.

Sometimes bishops disagree. When Nebraska Bishop Fabian Bruskewitz threatened to excommunicate Catholics in his diocese who belong to twelve organizations whose positions oppose Church teaching, the late Cardinal Joseph Bernardin of Chicago recognized that Bishop Bruskewitz had the right to use this canonical penalty, but added:

> "I do not favor such an approach. I favor stating clearly the teaching of the Church and the reasons for that teaching as well as the use of personal persuasion to change people's minds and hearts."

Bishops can also teach together in a region or in a national conference. For example, in February 1996, the Illinois Bishops took a strong stand in opposition to the death penalty. In July 1996, the U.S. Catholic Bishops officially opposed granting the legal status of marriage to relationships between persons of the same sex.

A big surprise for some Catholics is the fact that not all teachings of the Pope are infallible. According to Canon law, "No doctrine is understood to be infallibly defined unless it is clearly established as such." That means, a doctrine is declared infallible only when the Pope speaks *ex cathedra*, when an ecumenical council defines something as a matter of faith, or when all bishops in the world agree that a particular teaching is to be held definitively. In the course of history, there have been only two occasions when the Pope has promulgated doctrines as infallible, and he has always done so regarding matters long held in the popular piety or practice of the Church. The first is the doctrine of the Immaculate Conception (1854); the second is the doctrine of the Assumption of Mary (1950).

Another surprise for Catholics raised with the idea that

Church teaching is permanent and unchanging, were the radical changes after Vatican II. Some people are still confused:

> "I asked whether Baptists were eligible for salvation. A priest quoted Vatican II, which seemed to me to imply 'yes.' I used that quote with a guy I was arguing with and he quoted Pope Boniface VIII's *Unam Sanctam*, which says pretty clearly that to be saved you've got to accept the authority of the Pope. Who is right? Vatican II or Boniface VIII?" *Harold "Dan" Daniels*

The reality is that some Church teachings *have* changed over the centuries. As societies evolved and people grew in human understanding, some of the social, economic, moral and political teachings of the Church became obsolete. For example, the Church no longer teaches that slavery under certain circumstances may be morally justifiable. Catholics are no longer prohibited from lending money at interest. Pius XI's ban on Catholic membership in the YMCA is never mentioned, and of course, Boniface VIII's solemn proclamation that "There is but one holy, Catholic and Apostolic Church outside of which there is no salvation or remission of sins" was reinterpreted during the Second Vatican Council.

> "When I was growing up, it was easy to be a Catholic. You knew where first base was, and you knew how far you could wander without getting picked off. Now I'm not so sure." *N.D.*

Part of the problem stems from the recent media explosion and capabilities for instant global communication. In the past, Church teachings had a built-in maturation process. Rome would issue a document and by the time it worked its way into the pulpit, the teaching was refined in clear and simple terms. Today, the Associated Press runs a synopsis of the latest encyclical within minutes of its release. By dinner time, the network news has live interviews with priests, theologians and lay people, who may know nothing more about the teaching than what they read in the newspaper. Instant communication short-stopped the old maturation process, and some people attribute at least part of the confusion in the Church to this modern day phenomenon.

For example, in May 1996, the Catholic News Service reported on conflicting statements about sex education that were issued by two Vatican offices. Guidelines published by the Pontifical Council for the Family urged families to take control of teaching children about sex. Several months later, the Congregation for Catholic Education issued guidelines for sex education in Catholic schools. A conflict? No, said a Vatican spokesman, who pointed out that the documents each had a different emphasis which complement each other and serve as reflections on current issues.

While many people today struggle with the "rules" of the Church, Pope John Paul II insists that a mature understanding of our Catholic Christian faith and the teachings of the Church do not take away freedom, but encourage us toward responsible, mature freedom.

Moral theologian, Msgr. Angelo Caligiuri agrees. Before anyone can come to an understanding of authority or "rules," you must first accept the premise that freedom is not an absolute value. "Our society has gone off the deep end by advocating freedom at all cost," he insists,

> but it is responsible freedom that we should strive for. The real question is: *What are we free for?* Not: *What are we free from?* I don't think we've come to that understanding in our society. We say anything goes, and we hurt one another because we believe we have a right to our personal freedom. We've been led down the slippery slope of freedom as the absolute value, but it isn't.
>
> I'm free, but I have the responsibility of exercising that freedom in relation to other people. If I have a warped

notion of freedom and act accordingly, then I am going against the law of nature. For instance, I may want to rape someone right now, but if I do that I violate the other person's freedom and dignity.

I don't have to use my freedom. I can choose to limit my freedom for the common good. I can discipline myself. I can exercise my freedom according to a system of values. I can choose to act in the light of my Christian beliefs.

If you allow yourself to be formed by Catholic faith and tradition, there are significant values that the Catholic Church tells you are critical to your freedom. Call them rules if you want, but what you're putting into practice in real life decisions are values that you think are important for life — my life, your life, and the life of the world.

Father Gary Bagley, Youth Director for the Diocese of Buffalo, makes time to work with alienated Catholics because he realizes that many of them left the Church as teens and young adults, who were trying to break free from childhood "oughts" and "shoulds."

"The big issue for most of these people is: 'What does the Church say…' The point I try to make is that the Church says a lot of things. If the Bishops issue a statement saying, 'We're against capital punishment,' some people who are for capital punishment will say, 'Can I still be Catholic?' This is precisely why conscience is such a critical issue."

Our conscience serves as our value system, the standard by which we decide to act or not to act, and the basis on which our actions will be judged by God. The late Bishop Fulton J. Sheen called conscience an interior government. "It makes laws, it witnesses our actions in relation to the laws, and finally it judges us."

Conscience has nothing to do with "feelings." You may feel guilty because you ate a piece of chocolate cake or you may feel bad because you were too tired to go to the movies with a friend, but these things have nothing to do with moral choices or conscience. Likewise, you may not feel any guilt over hating your next door neighbor or sabotaging a co-worker by spreading false rumors, but harboring resentment and lying are certainly matters of morality and conscience.

The Church insists that it is the responsibility of every Catholic to form his or her own conscience. The *Catechism of the Catholic Church* states: "A well-formed conscience is upright and truthful. It formulates its judgments according to reason, in conformity with the true good willed by the wisdom of the Creator."

The formation of conscience is a life-long process that involves much more than picking up the newspaper, reading a synopsis of what the Pope said, and then saying "I agree" or "I disagree." Forming your conscience means taking the time to study Scripture and Church teachings; to continue your religious education through courses, books, tapes, or lectures; to pray for the guidance of the Holy Spirit; to seek advice from competent authorities; and to go through a private examination of conscience regularly. When forming your conscience, keep in mind it is never acceptable to do evil so that some good may result.

There are situations in which people end up with badly formed consciences. For example, a badly formed conscience might include:

- a person who follows the rules to the letter with no concern over how actions might affect other people.

- a person who finds excuses for everything and avoids guilt by refusing to accept personal responsibility.

- a person who has no moral structure and feels no guilt.

- a person who is too scrupulous and feels unjustified guilt about everything.

Conscience is our fundamental sense of right and wrong. Some of our most deeply ingrained, personal "rules" come from the depths of our own consciences, which the Church calls the voice of God echoing in each person and calling that person "to love and to do what is right and to avoid evil."

> "I believe God has told me some things are all right in ways so strong that no one from the local priest to the Pope could tell me I got it wrong." *Eilish Maura*

The Church has always upheld the sanctity of conscience:

- "He who acts against his conscience loses his soul." (Fourth Lateran Council, 1215)

- "It is better to perish in excommunication than to violate one's conscience." (St. Thomas Aquinas)

- "I shall drink... to Conscience first, and to the Pope afterwards." (Cardinal John Henry Newman)

- "If Newman places conscience above authority, he is not proclaiming anything new with respect to the constant teaching of the Church." (Pope John Paul II)

- "In the final analysis, conscience is inviolable and no person is to be forced to act in a manner contrary to his/her conscience, as the moral tradition of the Church attests." (*Human Life in Our Day*, U.S. Bishops Pastoral)

What does all of this mean for someone who is struggling with a particular "rule" of the Church? The bottom line is that you must take responsibility for your own conscience. Don't expect a priest to give you permission to reject Church teaching. He may not agree with the teaching himself, but he has no right to give you permission not to agree.

"I personally believe we will have married priests someday," admitted a priest who asked not to be identified. "I think one day we will have a different understanding of birth control, but I can't preach that and I can't allow that to be given in marriage instructions."

Likewise, no one in the Church has the right to judge you or condemn you for what you believe is right or wrong unless you take a public stand on an issue that is central to Catholic belief and try to convince others of your position.

This is not an easy process. For some it will be more difficult than for others, and throughout this book, specific matters of conscience will be examined in more detail. For now, let's just answer the initial question of who makes the rules by restating the Catholic teaching that ultimately, the "rules" all come from God speaking through Scripture, through Tradition, through nature, through the Pope and the Bishops, and through your own conscience. Whether you choose to accept or reject the "rules" depends on your faith and your understanding of how God is present in the world. In the next chapter, we'll look at a related question that surfaces often at Come Home programs: "How much do I have to believe?"

Chapter Notes

When asked in a recent survey: Thomas P. Sweetster, SJ, "The Parish: What Has Changed, What Remains?" *America*, February 17, 1996, pp. 6-7.

a prohibition against homicide...: *Catechism of the Catholic Church*, (hereafter CCC), New York: William H. Sadlier, Inc. 1994, p. 546, # 2266, # 2267.

Bishop Michael D. Pfeifer of San Angelo...: Catholic News Service, (hereafter CNS), April 16, 1996.

"I do not favor such an approach...": *Chicago Tribune*, April 12, 1996.

In February 1996, the Illinois Bishops took a strong stand: CNS, February 12, 1996.

In July 1996, the U.S. Catholic Bishops officially opposed: CNS, July 23, 1996.

The Pope and the bishops never originate new truths... : Vatican II, "Dogmatic Constitution on the Church," # 25.

"No doctrine is understood to be infallibly defined...": Code of Canon Law, canon 749.

"... the documents each had a different emphasis": Cindy Wooden, "Dueling Documents," CNS, May 10, 1996.

"to love and to do what is right...": CCC, p. 428, # 1776.

"It makes laws, it witnesses our actions...": Fulton J. Sheen, *From the Angel's Blackboard*, Liguori, Missouri: Triumph Books, 1995, p. 15.

"If Newman places conscience above authority...": Pope John Paul II, *Crossing the Threshold of Hope*, New York: Alfred J. Knopf, 1994, p. 191.

"A well-formed conscience is upright and truthful...": CCC, p. 440, # 1783.

CHAPTER 5

How Much Do You Have To Believe?

"Why should we come back? Why should we force our minds to believe in things that don't exist? The seeker must either submit to reason and walk away, but still live with the haunting memories. Or she must submit to the memories and live without reason." *A.F., Ohio*

"What does it mean to take something on faith? Do we have a choice about what we are willing to take on faith?" *Harold "Dan" Daniels*

"I'm having some problems with what I believe. How much do I have to swallow if I want to come back to the Catholic Church?" *J.D., New York*

Some people insist that in order to be Catholic you must blindly accept everything that the Catholic Church teaches. No questions. No doubts. No compromises.

Others say Catholics are supposed to question what the truth is and how we put the truth into action in our lives.

An interesting example of this dichotomy played itself out on the Internet during the winter of 1996, when a woman posted a message to Catholic subscribers on America Online saying that she felt as if God were drawing her back to the Catholic Church, but she had difficulty accepting some of the Catholic teachings. "Can I come back?" she wrote.

Thirty-nine people responded to her inquiry, and almost half said: "No. You can't come back unless you accept everything. Otherwise, you'll only cause trouble."

The other half disagreed, pointing out that some of the greatest saints struggled with what they believed. "We want you back," they said. "We would be richer having you with us than having you out there alone. Come and struggle with us."

For people who have fallen away from the Church and are thinking about coming back, the specter of this ongoing skirmish can run the gamut from frustrating to frightening. "How much do I have to believe?" they ask.

Father Andrew Greeley would tell you that in order to be Catholic "there are only a few things one has to believe, but those very strongly."

What are those few things? Essentially, Catholics believe in the person of Jesus Christ, son of God and son of Mary, true God and true man; they believe in the God of love whom Jesus reveals, and the Catholic faith community that developed under the guidance of the Holy Spirit. Jesus may never have said, "I'm going to make a Church with a Pope, bishops, and dioceses," but Catholics believe that the Holy Spirit dwells in the structure of the Church so the primacy of the Pope and the teaching authority of the Church are an important part of the Catholic belief system.

Look at the Apostles Creed, which was formulated as a summary of what the apostles taught. It is a personal profession of faith in the Trinity, in the Incarnation of Jesus Christ, his death, his resurrection, his ascension, and the promise of his second coming when he will judge the living and the dead. It also professes faith in the holy catholic Church, the communion of saints, the forgiveness of sins, the resurrection of the body and everlasting life.

Believing in something, even though you can't explain it and don't understand it, is called an assent of faith. It means that by an act of will you freely surrender your intellect and accept something as truth. If you're already starting to bristle at the thought of this, consider the fact that you make assents of faith in other areas of your life all the time without paying too much attention. If someone tells you they love you, there's no way you can prove or measure that love. You take it on faith. You trust that person.

In many ways, our lives are built on trust. We trust that other drivers will stop at red lights. We trust that food we eat in restaurants has not been poisoned. The contamination of over-the-counter drugs, the recent airplane disasters, and the terrorist bombings at the Oklahoma Federal Building and the World Trade Center are devastating because they shake our sense of trust.

The problem many people face with religion is that they don't want to take a creed or a dogma on faith or trust. They want proof. They want to understand it. "How could this possibly be true?" they ask.

There are, however, some elements of Catholicism that simply cannot be explained logically, scientifically or historically. They are mysteries passed down through the centuries from generation to generation. To try and unwrap the mystery of the Trinity, for instance, would mean that it would not be a mystery anymore. You would just explain it away. Some people say that mystery is an important part of our faith experience because it carries us into the unknown. If you had proof, there would be no need for faith.

The essence of faith is believing in Jesus Christ, who revealed truths about a loving and merciful God, about life, about death, about our relationships with other people and about ourselves. Catholic teaching on these matters is very explicit, and differs in some essential ways from the teachings of other Christian churches.

"There's a lot of confusion out there about Jesus and what he really taught," writes syndicated columnist Father John Catoir. "There are a lot of different answers but sooner or later you have to face the question, who are you going to believe? Either Christ was divine or he wasn't, either he has risen from the dead, or he hasn't."

The same holds for the Eucharist. Catholics believe that during the Mass, bread and wine are changed into the Body and Blood of Christ. Either you believe in the Real Presence of Christ in the Eucharist or you don't.

> "I never expected to come back to Catholicism. The major stumbling block was the Eucharist. The Catholics I knew had this mystical stuff going on that they could not explain and I could not fathom. The shift happened during a class I took on the Eucharist. I began to see that it is not just a wafer, it is the transubstantiated Body of Christ, and when we receive Communion, we share a meal as the Body of Christ." *Joe Hattick, Colorado Springs, Colorado*

Beyond these essential beliefs, the Catholic Church has official doctrines based on Scripture and Tradition, seven sacraments, a system of liturgies, and a body of official teachings on morality, justice, peace, and human rights. These teachings carry different levels of authority, and are not equally binding. Within this realm of what Catholics believe, there is "an order or hierarchy of truths, since [doctrines] vary in their relation to the foundation of the Christian faith." Topping the list are basic, unchangeable beliefs in the Trinity, the Incarnation, and the Resurrection. At the bottom of the list are Marian apparitions and personal revelations of Saints, which the Church says are worthy of belief, but not essential for salvation.

Historically, theologians used a ranking system that ranged from "Solemnly Defined Doctrine" to "Probable Opinion" because the Church recognized that every teaching was not divinely revealed. "Consequently, with regard to the Church's authoritative but non-defined teaching, there is at least a remote possibility of error," writes Richard R. Gillardetz. "Where such a remote possibility exists, the faithful cannot be asked to give an assent of faith."

Technically, no one can force you to believe anything that the Catholic Church teaches. Canon law states, "All persons are bound to seek the truth in matters concerning God and God's Church; by divine law they are also obligated and have the right to embrace and to observe the truth which they have recognized. Persons cannot ever be forced by anyone to embrace the Catholic faith against their conscience."

> "On the one hand, it's really difficult to draw a hard line between what a Catholic MUST believe and what is 'imprudent' to disbelieve. On the other hand, why believe something at all?" *Harold "Dan" Daniels*

The real issue here is not a matter of what you have to believe as much as it is a matter of how your faith is growing and developing. Mark Twain's definition of faith as "believing what you know ain't so," is not real faith.

Faith is a lifelong process of searching for truth, finding truth, committing ourselves to truth, and constantly shaping our lives to conform to truth. Father Mark Link, SJ, suggests that the faith journey begins in childhood with stories passed on by parents and teachers. Childhood faith tends to be very black and white without any room for doubt. You are Catholic in the same way that you may be Italian or Irish. It is part of your family, your heritage, your culture. As adolescents and young adults, people go through a transition period when doubts and questions kill off childhood faith so you can make an adult faith commitment based on the conviction that this is what you want to believe and how you want to live your life.

> "I am 15, and up until now, I have accepted everything I was taught about religion, but recently I have begun questioning my beliefs. It doesn't make sense to me that I should believe in the God that my parents believe in just

because they are my parents. When I pray at night, I don't really know who I'm praying to." *Michael Gillespie*

"The death of our childhood faith makes us feel sick of heart — even guilty," Father Link says. "This is unfortunate for our faith is simply going through an important growth stage."

According to Father Link, the transition process takes place on three levels:

- In the mind, where we begin our search for truth amid questions and doubts as to the nature of God and the various tenets of the Catholic faith.

- In the heart, where we search for the real meaning of love in our feeble attempt to discover the truth that God is love.

- In the soul, where we open ourselves to experiences of God that renew our faith and instill in us a willingness to make a personal commitment to a new way of life.

Father John Catoir remembers traveling to California with friends during his college years. "They had rejected Catholicism and they tried mightily to unsettle me in my beliefs. They threw every objection at me they could think of, and I tried to defend what I believed. By the end of the summer I may have weakened their confidence, but I know they shook mine. I was emotionally drained and ready to chuck the whole religious issue once and for all. I went to see Father Jim McCoy. He had a deep untrembling intellectual center. He handled my questions and objections calmly and without difficulty. Gradually I began to realize that it wasn't so much a matter of getting answers, which I did get from him, rather it was a matter of growing and maturing in judgment."

Some people, however, seem to get stuck in this transition period, and never move out of a state of perpetual doubts and questions:

"I can't call myself a Catholic, and yet, somehow, I can't walk away either." *A.F., Ohio*

Some people choose to believe only what they want to believe:

"I don't necessarily want to be Catholic again. I want to find a place or group that understands and accepts my beliefs, not because I'm right or wrong, but because it's my opinion, formed by learning and experience." *C. Bruce Santore II, Ohio*

St. Augustine observed, however, that if you choose to believe only what you like and you reject what you don't like, "it is not the Gospel you believe, but yourself."

Sometimes a person may want to believe, but without a strong inner experience of God the desire is not enough to sustain a faith commitment. Many people, who memorized every word of the *Baltimore Catechism* as children, for instance, fell away from the Church when some of the external practices, such as not eating meat on Friday, were changed. Their "faith" was not centered in a religious experience of God, but in a set of rules, and when the rules changed, they felt as if their faith dissolved.

"My questions turned to anger. Why was I taught all this stuff if it isn't true? I didn't bother to research and seek answers. I just came to my own conclusion that none of it was true. My anger was then focused on those who had taught me, primarily the Church. I began to scoff whenever I heard an announcement of the Church's position on anything. My feelings toward the Church became almost hostile, and I began to view the Church as tyrannical. Eventually, my anger was focused not just at the Catholic Church, but at all organized religion." *Julie Richard, Kansas City, Missouri*

Psychologist C.G. Jung once wrote: "Theology does not help those who are looking for the key, because theology demands faith, and faith cannot be made: it is in the truest sense a gift of grace."

There's nothing more frustrating to people who are seeking answers than to be told that they will not find what they are looking for until God gives them some elusive gift. The truth is that you already received "the gift" at baptism, but it may have been laying dormant because you never recognized the presence of the Holy Spirit, "who moves the heart and converts it to God, who opens the eyes of the mind and makes it easy for all to accept and believe the truth."

Sometimes, a person will feel a movement of God in the depths of the soul, which begins a process called conversion. "To be converted, to be regenerated, to receive grace, to experience religion, to gain an assurance, are so many phrases which denote the process, gradual or sudden, by which a self hitherto divided, and consciously wrong, inferior and unhappy, becomes unified and consciously right, superior and happy, in consequence of its firmer hold upon religious realities," explains psychologist William James.

C.G. Jung would agree: "No matter what the world thinks about religious experience, the one who has it possesses a great treasure, a thing that has become for him a source of life, meaning, and beauty, and that has given a new splendor to the world and to mankind… Is there, as a matter of fact, any better truth about ultimate things than the one that helps you live?"

Thomas Merton describes his conversion experience as a deep interior impulsion:

> I will not easily forget how I felt that day. First, there was this sweet, strong, gentle, clean urge in me which said: "Go to Mass! Go to Mass!" It was something quite new and strange, this voice that seemed to prompt me, this firm, growing interior conviction of what I needed to do. It had a suavity, a simplicity about it that I could not easily account for. And when I gave in to it, it did not exalt over me, and trample me down in its raging

haste to land on its prey, but it carried me forward serenely and with purposeful direction.

What if you feel that you are being drawn back to the Church, but you aren't sure what you believe?

Msgr. Angelo Caligiuri, who has worked with alienated Catholics, advises people to concentrate on the realization that God is working in your life:

> It's God that brought you to this point, so whatever you're feeling about specific issues is important, but not critical right now. Get in touch with the mystery of God in your life. Nurture that in whatever way you know how. Knowledge is important in terms of Church teaching, but more important is your relationship with God, who may be drawing you into a profound conversion experience. Move with the grace of the moment.
>
> At some point on your journey back, you will have to start addressing specific issues. You can't run away from them. But first, you should affirm this attraction to Catholic identity that you are feeling. I don't think it's important at the first moment to sign a declaration of faith. The important thing is that you are here. God has brought you here. God is working in your life.

Many returning Catholics find that while intellectual struggles with dogmas and Church teachings were the source of their alienation, very often their healing took place on a spiritual level.

> "No, we haven't laboriously studied out all the doctrine or answered the questions we had. We just felt God calling us there, and the first time we went, the Holy Spirit surrounded us with the sweetest feeling of love and warmth... and that was all the 'investigation' we needed. If God says so, do it. And do it without reservation. Then everything else will fall into place." *Janice Haber, Guthrie, Oklahoma*

"Having been away from God bitterly and distantly for some time, I can certainly share my experience. Ultimately, it is profoundly and simply a choice. I choose to believe in God; or I choose not to believe in God. Once I choose to believe in God, then I choose the method by which I experience that choice — through Church, tradition, ritual, exclusivity, inclusively, etc. In the end the language of God is silence. So, in the quietude of my own soul, I examine my faith, my belief, my choice. For it is there, in that final, miraculous moment between this life and whatever is next, no matter how many people stand at my death bed, I alone will silently, finally know."
Clyde Pearce

Chapter Notes

"there are only a few things one has to believe...": John J. Delaney, Editor, *Why Catholic?*, New York: Doubleday & Company, Inc., 1979, p. 61.

"There are a lot of different answers...": Fr. John Catoir, "Why I am a Catholic," *The Catholic Evangelist*, January/February, 1986.

"an order or hierarchy of truths...": CCC, p. 28, # 90.

"Where such a remote possibility exists...": Richard R. Gillardetz, "Proclaiming the Catholic Faith," *Commonweal*, February 9, 1996, pp. 14-18.

"All persons are bound to seek the truth...": Code of Canon Law, canon 748.

"believing what you know ain't so...": Mark Twain, *Mark Twain's Notebook*, edited by Albert Bigelow Paine, New York: Harper Brothers, 1935, p. 237.

"The death of our childhood faith...": Mark Link, SJ, *Path Through Catholicism*, Allen, Texas: Tabor Publishing, 1991, p. 4.

"Theology does not help those who are looking...": C.G. Jung, *Psychological Reflections*, Princeton, New Jersey: Princeton University Press, 1970, p. 351.

"who moves the heart and converts it to God...": Vatican II, *Dei Verbum*, 5, November, 1965.

"To be converted...": William James, *The Varieties of Religious Experience*, New York: The Modern Library, 1929, p. 186.

"No matter what the world thinks...": Jung, *Psychological Reflections*, p. 350.

"I will not easily forget...": Thomas Merton, *The Seven Storey Mountain*, New York: Harcourt Brace & Co., 1948, p. 206.

CHAPTER 6

Dealing with Doubts

"I quietly doubt inside. People think I am 100% Catholic, but I see so many things in the Catholic Church that don't reflect love and acceptance and dignity for all human beings." *D.S.*

"I am a medical student and I am struggling with terrible doubts about God. I can't prove that God exists and I can't prove that he doesn't exist." *T.P.*

"I left the Church because of doubts. Who was Jesus? Did he really exist? If God is so wonderful, why do bad things happen? Is there really a heaven? What was there REALLY to believe? No one really knows what happens to us after death, so what difference does it make?" *Julie Richard, Kansas City, Missouri*

When Father Tom Doyle tells people who struggle with faith that it's good to have doubts, they are usually dumbfounded. A priest saying doubts are good?

"Think about it," he says. "The opposite of faith is not doubts. The opposite of faith is denial. When you doubt something, it means you don't have enough knowledge to resolve your question. Your natural reaction is to try and resolve the doubt. That's good."

One of the Scripture quotes Father Tom uses is the story

of the apostles in the boat in the middle of the lake when Jesus starts walking to them on the water. They are frightened. They don't know who it is. Peter finally recognizes Christ. He jumps in and starts walking across the water. As long as Peter focuses on Jesus, he is all right, but when he looks down and realizes that he is walking on water, he starts to sink. The Lord reaches out and saves him.

"Peter doubted, but he didn't drown. You won't drown, either," Father Tom promises.

Then he asks people to imagine that they are standing by a frozen pond. Suppose you want to get to the other side. You don't know if the ice is thick enough to support your weight. You have doubts. What are you going to do? You might take a stick and poke the ice. You might take a rock and throw it on the pond. You might take your foot and put a little weight on the ice. Then you might take another step. You might continue to test that ice step by step until you've walked across.

"It's the same with faith," he says. "When you have doubts and you begin to resolve those doubts, they eventually lead you to truth. But you have to keep testing. Before you can know the truth, you have to doubt, and doubt well."

Psychologist C.G. Jung would agree. "Wherever belief reigns, doubt lurks in the background. But thinking people welcome doubt: it serves them as a valuable stepping-stone to better knowledge."

If we examine some of the doubts expressed by people who have been away from the Church, we find that they fall into several categories:

• **Doubts about God**

> "After my wife died in a tragic accident, I returned to the Church following a 20-year absence. I went to Mass every day, read the Bible, and even paid a priest $50 an hour for counseling. Six months later, I walked away, not because I disagree with the Church's teachings on celibacy, women

priests, abortion, or anything else. I just quit believing. I have no confidence that my 'life' will extend one second beyond the ceasing of my bodily function. I love the story of Christ and admire his teachings, but I have no certainty of the existence of God." *J.C.*

There is no empirical evidence for the existence of God, but likewise, there is no absolute proof that God does not exist. Father Andrew Greeley suggests that when some people question God's existence, what they are really questioning is not God, but the caricature of a distant, punishing God that was imposed on them as children: "To put the matter differently, the God in whom they were taught to believe is not a God in whom it is worth believing. Even God himself would reject that kind of God."

One man in the Come Home program made a list of all the images he had of God:

> "Then I crossed off everything that I could not accept like God as an old man with a white beard who speaks in thunder and threatens to destroy the world, or God as a cosmic policeman waiting for you to do something wrong so he can zap you, or God as a Santa Claus who rewards good kids and gives coal to bad kids, or God the great puppeteer in the sky who jerks people's strings. When I crossed off these things, I had nothing left on my list."
> *D.L., New York*

If you've discarded all of your negative images of God, you can begin to search for the true God by asking God for help. What Charles de Foucald termed his "strange prayer," consisted in repeating the words: "My God, if you exist, make your presence known to me." This kind of prayer is in itself an admission that you are open to believing in God's existence. You can also explore new images of a loving God. Father John Powell, SJ, uses the image that God is like the sun, never moving, never changing, always pouring out warmth and light. "We can stand under the sun, share its gifts of warmth and light, or we can leave it," Father Powell suggests. "We can even lock ourselves in the dungeons of darkness. But the sun does not go out because we have left it. In the same way, we can leave God, but he does not change. He only loves us. We are free to reject the warmth and light of his love. If we do, we grow dark and cold and can even fall into spiritual death. But we are always free, and even when we are languishing in the dark, we know we can always go back into the warm light of God's love."

You can look for God in nature, in Scripture, in the people around you and in the stories that they tell. Father Avery Dulles, SJ, a theology professor at Fordham University, points out that theologically it is correct to say that the desire to find God is proof that God is drawing us to himself.

"If I were asked this question about finding faith or finding God," says Anne Carr, BVM, Professor of Theology at the Divinity School of the University of Chicago, "I would guess that the questioner already had a desire for God that entailed a kind of implicit faith."

"There were times when I doubted the existence of God. It's taken me ten years to figure out that God is absolute in my life." *Frank Barbarossa, M.D., Amherst, New York*

• **Doubts about God's presence**

"There are many times when I don't feel God's presence within like I used to. I'm not sure what I believe anymore. I feel as if I've lost my faith." *F.S.*

Classical theology tells us that feelings of spiritual dryness are God's way of moving us into a deeper relationship with him. It's easy to love someone when you have good feelings about that person or when good things are happening in your life. However, when the person you love goes away for a while or when illness or some disaster disturbs the positive flow of the relationship, you are forced to move beyond your own "feelings" and focus on the commitment you made to that relationship. If you really love that person, your commitment will grow stronger when a trial enters your life. Likewise, it's easy to love God when you have all sorts of positive spiritual feelings, but when the feelings go flat, God may be calling you to deepen your faith and your trust.

> "I have become a sometimes churchgoer. When I am there, I do feel very peaceful and everything seems to be okay. But when I try to carry that feeling outside it somehow becomes lost. I don't know if I've lost faith in God or in man. I only know that I do keep on praying." *S.N., Ridgewood, New Jersey*

• **Doubts about God's forgiveness**

> "I left because of a sin I committed over 13 years ago. I just felt that I couldn't be forgiven. I was actually afraid that I would be turned away if I tried to come back." *V.F.*

People who doubt God's unconditional love and mercy usually cannot forgive themselves for something they have done, so they project their own burden onto God and wonder how God could possibly forgive them. It becomes a vicious cycle that drags them into despair and hopelessness. Sometimes these negative attitudes about forgiveness stem from childhood when parents failed to separate the fact that an *action* is wrong or bad, not the person. Some people still have a nagging voice inside of themselves saying, "You're bad. Nothing you do is right. You'll never be any good."

Some people carry the burden of deep, dark, shameful secrets for years. It might have been an abortion, or a single homosexual experience, or an episode of infidelity, or vandalism, or some act of revenge. These people feel terribly guilty, but in order to accept God's forgiveness, they have to let go of that guilt and negativity. They have to change their image of

God from harsh and unforgiving to loving and merciful. They have to get rid of their image of themselves as intrinsically bad and unforgivable. They have to begin to see themselves as good people who make mistakes.

Father Gary Bagley tells the story of a teenager, who sank into a deep depression and refused to speak. No one could break through to him and depression began to turn into despair. Then one day, the boy went outside to play basketball, and a little while later, he bounded back into the house shouting, "He's alive! I didn't kill him!" This boy had been in a street fight several months before, and during the fight, he thought he had killed his rival. Guilt, fear and shame pulled him into the abyss of himself until he saw the other boy on the basketball court. The boy was alive. He hadn't killed him.

"I think that some of you are afraid that you killed something," Father Gary tells people at Come Home sessions. "But I want you to know that whatever you think you did is not that bad. You didn't kill anything. It's still alive."

• **Doubts about being a "good" Catholic**

> "I went to public school, and we had religious instructions during release time. I always felt as if I wasn't as good as the kids who went to Catholic school. I just drifted away from the Church, but now my daughter should be attending classes for First Communion. I know I should come back, but I don't know where I fit or if I ever could be a 'good' Catholic." *M.B.*

In some parts of the country, particularly where the Catholic school system was strong, there exists a kind of inferiority complex among people who went to public schools. It is very subtle, but it's very real, and does not stem from anything that these people did, but rather from things that were said or done to make them think that they were not as "good" as the Catholic school kids.

"I learned NEXT TO NOTHING in CCD classes. There are so many things I felt ignorant about and did not have the courage to ask anyone." *Margaret Sullivan, Massachusetts*

Father Ron Pecci, OFM, remembers being told that he couldn't be an altar server because he went to public school:

I also remember a party we had during religion class in fourth or fifth grade for a boy, who was transferring from the public school into the Catholic school. The nun told us his parents loved him so much that they were going to let him go to Catholic school now, and we had a party to celebrate. Those kinds of things made you feel like a second class Catholic.

When we made our First Communion and Confirmation, the Catholic school children marched first, and then the public school kids marched behind them. It was two separate groups, and very often the public school kids hadn't been adequately prepared with prayers or songs, so we felt even more uncomfortable.

I'm sure they figured that Catholic education was good and they needed to do everything they could to bring children into the Catholic school, but they laid a certain amount of guilt and rejection on kids who did not go to Catholic school.

We had classes on Wednesday afternoons, and we were always accused of stealing erasers or books. If desks or papers on the board were marked up, we were held responsible. I don't ever remember doing anything like that. Maybe some other kids did, but I always felt that we were looked down upon. I felt that they didn't care all that much for us. Some kids may not have realized it on a conscious level, but it sent a subtle yet powerful message.

Father Ron encourages other "public school kids" to reject those painful memories from the past because the message was wrong: You were not second class Catholics. Don't let doubts about what you know or where you fit stand in the way of your adult faith experience. In God's eyes, you are just as important and lovable as anyone else — no matter where you went to school. Find a place for yourself, and don't ever allow anyone to tell you that you are not as "good" as someone else. If you feel that your religious education was lacking, study, read, listen to tapes, take advantage of the adult education courses in your parish. Don't allow a negative message from the past to affect your relationships with God or the Church.

• **Doubts about doubts**

> "I can't understand why it is so easy for my mother and my sisters to believe and it is so hard for me. I struggle, while they just seem to accept everything peacefully without any questions or doubts." *P.E.G.*

"Faith," says Father Andrew Greeley, "is not so much a matter of intelligence as it is docility to the signs of grace that abound all around us in the world, an openness to the influence of God as God reveals himself in the works of nature and in the human beings who love us."

Some people have a high degree of faith and it's easy for them to be trusting and open. They see God working in everyone and everything. Other people are constantly questioning, doubting, challenging, searching. Maybe it's due to different temperaments or personalities. Maybe it's due to different attitudes or ways of looking at life. Maybe it's tied to our ability to give and accept love. Sometimes doubts arise because a person is struggling to find purpose and meaning in life.

Father John Powell, SJ, tells the story of a young atheist in his theology class, who struggled to find God after he was diagnosed with terminal cancer. Shortly before the young man died, he told Father Powell, "Only when I opened myself in love to those around me did God come through the door of the heart I had left open."

Sometimes doubts help to strip away old forms of faith and bring us to new levels of faith and understanding. Sometimes doubts lead us to what we really believe about ourselves.

The late Father Henri Nouwen admitted that for most of his life he struggled to find God, to know God and to love God, but gradually, he came to realize that the question is not *How am I to find God, to know God, and to love God?* but *How am I to let myself be found, known, and loved by him?* "Questions like these raise a real issue: that of my own self concept. Can I accept that I am worth looking for? Do I believe that there is a real desire in God to simply be with me?"

• **Doubts about Catholic dogma**

"What if you find out that there are dogmas like the Immaculate Conception and Assumption that you can't accept? Can I be Catholic?" *B.L.*

Most people don't deny dogmas, but they sometimes question them or conclude that these teachings aren't as important to them as the central teachings about the life of Jesus Christ. The doctrines about Mary are certainly important to the Church, and since both dogmas were defined as infallible teachings, Catholics are expected to make an assent of faith, even if they struggle with the actual teaching.

Some people say, "How could this possibly be true? How can I convince myself that these things actually happened?" The answer is: You can't. You may never understand these teachings, and you may never be free from doubts about them. Through an act of will, you can accept the fact that the Church teaches that these dogmas are infallible truths whether you understand them or not.

Father Richard P. McBrien, a theology professor from the University of Notre Dame, explains that since strongly worded anathemas were attached to these dogmas, it is certainly possible that open rejection of the dogmas would be an indication that someone intended to separate from full communion with the Catholic Church:

> "A person might, for example, reject these definitions precisely because they are papal actions. That person might believe the Petrine office has no necessary place in the life and mission of the Church for the benefit of the Church universal. A person might also reject any place for Mary in the Christian dispensation and the Catholic tradition. Such views would effectively disengage one from the Catholic tradition and the community which embodies it. This is not to say, on the other hand, that a faithful and committed Catholic could not question the process by which these dogmas were formulated."

If you feel as if you are plagued with questions and doubts, make a list of all those things. Once you have identified your main concerns, you can begin to investigate. As you begin to resolve some of your doubts, you may find that new doubts surface. It's important to remember that you can't have faith without doubts.

Doubts help you learn, but sometimes doubts force you to learn the hard way. For example, you can tell a child, "Don't touch the stove. It's hot." Some kids will stay away, but other kids are going to test you, and they're going to get burned. In the process they learn that the stove really *is* hot!

Likewise, if someone had a bad experience with a priest or a nun, they may begin to doubt all priests and nuns. But once you make contact with a priest or a nun who is open, compassionate and wants to help, it begins the healing process. You still may have doubts about nuns and priests, but you've discovered that not all nuns and priests fit the pattern of your doubts.

Dealing with doubt always involves risk. In order to resolve your doubts, you have to step out of your fears and seek answers. Some people, who grew up in an era when the Church was strict and demanding, fear that they will be scolded, humiliated or turned away if they go to a priest. Instead, they turn to other Catholics, who may not know the correct answer. When you do that, you run the risk of getting wrong information, which could lead you into doubts about something that is not even true.

> "My husband left me and my relatives told me that as soon as my divorce papers were finalized that I was automatically excommunicated and I couldn't receive Communion anymore. I stayed away from the Church for three years before I found out that it wasn't true. I was not excommunicated." *A.T., New York*

This kind of bad information runs rampant among Catholics. If you have a serious question about your faith or some Church policy, check it out with a source that is reliable. Call the Chancery. Call a Catholic hospital and ask to talk to the chaplain. Call a Catholic college. Take an adult education course at a Catholic parish. Go to the library and look up your question in a Catholic encyclopedia or the Code of Canon Law.

> "I'd love to tell you that I had some wonderful revelation that helped me, but I didn't. What did happen was a slow nagging to be back where I belonged." *Julie Richard, Kansas City, Missouri*

As Father Tom Doyle suggests, when you begin to examine your doubts, you will find that your faith is still there, but your doubts kept it suppressed and never allowed it to develop. As your faith grows, you will start to discover spiritual insights. Your mind will begin to grasp a greater understanding of things that are beyond your senses, and you may begin to see that the invisible world of the Spirit is very real. It's almost as if you become a different person. You start to function on a whole different level. You become more accepting of other people and of yourself, more able to forgive, and better able to experience God's forgiveness.

"I came back to the Church three years ago. Not every question was resolved, but God welcomed me back with all of my doubts. And yes, it has changed my life." *E.G.*

Chapter Notes

"Wherever belief reigns...": C.G. Jung, *Psychological Reflections*, edited by Jolande Jacobi and R.F.C. Hull, Princeton, New Jersey: Princeton University Press, 1970, p. 354.

"To put the matter differently...": Andrew M. Greeley, *The Catholic Why? Book*, Chicago: St. Thomas More Press, 1983, p. 52.

"We can stand under the sun...": John Powell, SJ, *Through the Eyes of Faith*, Allen, Texas: Tabor Publishing, 1992, pp. 93-94.

Father Avery Dulles, SJ...: James Martin, "How Can I Find God?" *America*, September 30, 1995, pp. 12-21.

"If I were asked this question about finding faith...": *Ibid.*

"Faith," says Father Andrew Greeley...: Andrew M. Greeley, *The Catholic Why? Book*, p. 52.

"Only when I opened myself in love...": John Powell, SJ, *Through the Eyes of Faith*, p. 13.

"Questions like these...": Henri J. Nouwen, *The Return of the Prodigal Son*, New York: Doubleday, 1992, p. 101.

"A person might, for example...": Richard P. McBrien, *Catholicism*, San Francisco: Harper Collins Publishers, 1989, pp. 1102-1103.

CHAPTER 7

Mad at God and Holding a Grudge

"My husband left me after 38 years of marriage. I'm angry at him, but I'm also angry at God for allowing this to happen." *T.C., Pennsylvania*

"When I found out my son died in a fluke accident, I remember thinking, 'No!; this is a nightmare.' But it was true, and when I saw him lying in the casket, I wanted to die. Then I got angry. I was so angry at God for taking him away from me. I felt as if I hated God." *E.L., New York*

"When I was growing up, our lives were hell on earth. My father was an abusive alcoholic, and he terrorized my mother and all of us kids. I know for a fact that my mother refused to leave him because a priest told her that it would be a sin and she would burn in hell for breaking up the family. He said this was the cross God gave her to carry. Well, I'm sorry. I can't go along with that kind of a God. We were all being abused by a sick man and no one did anything to stop it." *M.M.*

"It's okay to be angry at God," Father David LiPuma tells people. "It's okay to say: *'I'm angry because you took this person away from me.' 'I'm angry because this person is sick.' 'I'm angry because you allowed this to happen.' 'I'm angry because someone hurt me very badly.' 'I'm angry because it feels as if my life is falling apart.'*

55

It's good to say those things out loud. God's shoulders are big-ger than we can ever imagine. He can handle it."

Father LiPuma understands how it feels to be angry at God. When he was in his first year of the minor seminary, his mother died. A few months later, his father died from a mas-sive heart attack. "I stood in that hospital room and I screamed at God," he recalls. "I was out of control. My brothers, who are kind of nominal Catholics, were the ones who calmed me down. I was so angry. It wasn't fair. I was giving my life to God, and God was taking away the people closest to me."

In looking back, Father LiPuma realizes that after the ini-tial outburst, he did not allow himself enough time to work through his anger.

Part of the problem of being angry at God is that you feel so hurt and so deeply wounded, but on some level, you tell yourself that there is something intrinsically wrong with get-ting angry at God. Instead of dealing with your anger, you try to bury your feelings. But suppressed anger does not go away. It festers, and you have to use a certain amount of emotional energy to keep it buried. Sometimes, the suppressed anger manifests itself as depression, or nervous tension, or self-pity or a victim mentality. Sometimes, people try to deaden the pain with pills, alcohol, drugs, sex, or some other compulsive behav-ior. Sometimes, the smoldering anger explodes in angry out-bursts over things that are completely unrelated.

Anger is simply an emotional response to something that you perceive as an injustice. Whether the injustice is real or imagined, you still feel anger, and ultimately you are going to have to deal with it.

"That's why it's important to talk about your feelings," Father LiPuma insists. "It's only when you can open up and let the anger drain out that you begin to heal. You need to find someone that you can be totally yourself with, someone you can talk to, someone who is not going to try to answer what you're feeling or try to fix your feelings. You don't need someone preaching to you. You need someone to listen with an open heart."

"I called a priest and asked if I could come in and talk. That's all I wanted to do. I really didn't want anything more than that. It was a very emotional experience. I didn't realize how angry I was. We spent a couple of hours talking about my whole life and everything that had gone on. He just listened, and then he suggested that we pray together. It helped me to let it all go."
C.D., New York

Sister Margaret Krantz, FMDC, a certified bereavement minister, agrees that people have to talk about their feelings. In dealing with grieving families, she meets many people who have fallen away from the Church. Some have carried angry feelings toward God for years, and the reasons usually stem from some kind of loss.

Divorce, for example, is like the death of a marriage, the death of dreams, the death of a commitment, and it is often accompanied by feelings of anger, rejection, betrayal, guilt and immense loneliness.

"I struggled with divorce after 29 years of marriage. Although I was the one who decided that we were at an end, I suffered extreme spiritual death."
Lenne Shields-Orona, Des Moines, Iowa

Some people are furious at God and the Church over an annulment they feel was granted unjustly.

"My marriage was nullified because my husband could not remain faithful to me. I was very angry for a long time. I am trying to put that anger in the past. My daughter tells me that the annulment has consumed my life and it is time for me to be whole again." *B.J., Florida*

People struggle with anger at God over a debilitating injury, a serious physical or mental illness, an act of violence against an innocent person, the death of a child, the loss of a job, a forced early retirement, a failed business venture, a deep disappointment caused by a friend or family member, an unexplainable accident, or some natural tragedy that destroys homes or lives.

"The process of working through any kind of loss is essentially a grieving process," Sister Margaret explains. "At first, you go through denial. You refuse to accept that this happened. Then you experience anger. You begin to ask: 'Why me? What have I done to deserve this?' Depression follows, and finally acceptance, readjusting, recovery and healing. When people feel angry at God, I tell them that this is a normal stage in the grieving process. I also assure them that we're safe when we get angry at God because God doesn't retaliate. God is always there loving us no matter how we feel. If you can turn to God in your anger, you will begin to be healed — not totally — because some things that happen in life you never forget. Some things will always hurt, but the sharpness of the pain will go away, and you will reach a point where life will have meaning again."

Some people have a hard time turning to God. When Sister Joyce Rupp, OSM, began teaching a course entitled "Praying Our Good-byes," a young widow, who could not forgive God after her husband's death, advised Sister Joyce not to naively assume that all people receive strength from their faith. It's hard for some people to turn to God as a source of strength when they see God as the source of their suffering. Some people believe that if you're good, God will take care of you. If you're not good, bad things will happen because God is going to punish you.

"You might think the world operates this way, but it never does," says Father Richard Zajac, a hospital chaplain. "If a tornado comes, God doesn't redirect that tornado around your house and hit your neighbor instead because you are better than your neighbor. God doesn't look in his computer and see whom he can jolt. Many times bombs fly, bones break, people get sick and people die with no discrimination as to who deserves it and who doesn't."

Anyone accustomed to rationalizing their problems will find this reality difficult to accept. When bad things happen, some people want to know why. They assume that if they knew the reason, acceptance would be easier. The problem is, in most cases, there is no answer.

> "When my daughter died from acute leukemia, I exploded at the priest. I wanted to know why. The priest told me that we all question why the innocent suffer and why suffering is not equally distributed, but he said God never explains why. I don't know why that was comforting to me. I keep thinking that it should make me even madder, but I started thinking that maybe there's a reason for things that I don't understand." *K.S., New York*

"It is the great sin of some religious people to think that there is a satisfactory answer to a tragedy of this sort, and to tell the afflicted parents such dreadful things as, 'At least you have the other two,' or 'God must have needed her,' or 'She's in heaven now,' or 'It must have been her time,'" writes John Garbey. "In the book of Job we find that God rebukes Job's comforters. In effect, God says to Job: 'I know what I am doing and you do not and cannot.'"

What usually does help is prayer, but the great irony is that people who are angry at God often find it impossible to pray. They feel no tenderness, no comfort, no consolation.

"If you're angry at God, keep fighting with him because it's in that dialogue that you will come to some peace with it," says Father LiPuma. "It is okay to tell God what we think or how we feel — even if we are angry. That's called prayer, and it's some of the best prayer because you are speaking honestly from your heart. God can handle it."

Sister Joyce Rupp agrees: "Sometimes we may be 'too nice' with God. We hide our true feelings because we do not want to shock or offend God or have God think ill of us. We do not want to admit that we are capable of such feelings. We need to let God hear our cry and our distress. God knows it anyhow! Let God hear our anger and our confusion, our frustrations and our disorientation. Let God know that we wish things would change for us or that things were different."

Sometimes people are angry at God because their prayers aren't answered in the ways they would have liked. Father John Catoir faced this kind of faith crisis when his mother died during his second year in the seminary. "I was praying so hard for her to live," he recalls.

> I thought it would be my mother's great desire to see me ordained and I couldn't understand why God did not answer my prayers. One of the major pillars of my faith was the faith and confidence I had that if I prayed hard and really believed the Lord would be there for me. When this didn't happen, it opened up the possibility that there may be other situations when I would need God's help and he would not appear.
> It took about five or six months until I began to think of it from a different perspective. My mother was in pain. She was suffering. What advantage would there be for her to go through two more years of agony? She could see my ordination from another base. Maybe she would be applauded in heaven in a way that she wouldn't be on earth. It was a matter of trusting that God knows what is really best.

Father LiPuma agrees. In spite of all the pain he endured, he now believes that some good came out of his parents' deaths. "I still miss them and I still want them," he says. "That feeling never goes away. But the whole experience made me realize that my decision to become a priest was not for them. It was for God. I'm not saying God took them away because he wanted me to be totally focused on him, but I realized after they died that I couldn't do this for anybody else. I also have a different feeling about my parents. It has given me great hope in the resurrection. I'm not afraid to die because I know that someday I'll see them again. I believe that in many ways my life has been blessed by the two of them being with God. I really feel that lots of times in my life there has been a watchful protection that I kind of rely on."

"Twenty years after my son died, I woke up in the middle of the night and it was almost as if God said to me, 'I was with you when your son died and you were in church crying. That was me. I was with you.' It was so real. It wasn't a voice. It was a deep inner knowledge that came to me in the middle of the night. So now I know that God has always been there for me. He's here now. He gives me peace." *E.Q., New York*

Chapter Notes

"When Sister Joyce Rupp, OSM, began teaching a course...": Joyce Rupp, OSM, *Praying Our Good-byes*, Notre Dame: Ave Maria Press, 1995, p. 19.

"It is the great sin of some religious people...": John Garbey, "When a Child Dies," *Commonweal*, March 24, 1995, p. 8.

"Sometimes we may be 'too nice' with God...": Rupp, p. 85.

CHAPTER 8

Are You Listening, Lord?

"I've been away from the Church for 15 years, and I don't know how to pray. I remember some of the prayers the nuns taught us, but they seem so rote. The old formulas just aren't doing it. I don't feel God's presence. I have to admit that it seems kind of ironic that I should be asking where God is when for the past 15 years he was probably asking the same question about me!" *C.M., New York*

"I hated the job I had working in a freezer nine hours a day. I prayed to God for a better job, but nothing seemed to be happening. I was starting to think once again that my prayers were in vain, and then I got a call from someone who wanted to make me a job offer. I think God heard my prayers after all." *Joe MacKay, Seattle*

"I had an abortion a year ago. I was a pro-choice feminist at the time and did not think I was doing anything wrong. I still understand my reasons for the choice I made, but I was not prepared for the consequences. I felt that God turned his back on me. I couldn't pray." *C.P.*

When Carol Samuelson of Jamestown, New York could no longer resist the spiritual pull she was feeling, she decided to take the easy way and watch religious television shows rather than go back to church. On one of the programs someone said,

"If you're thinking about coming back to the Church, pray. Even if it is only for ten minutes a day, pray."

> I went to my bedroom and stood both literally and figuratively on the threshold of the room thinking about how I was about to admit that I believed God actually exists. I thought about how the act of kneeling itself, without saying a thing, was an acknowledgment that God exists and that He is greater than I. I wasn't sure whether I was ready for that. I decided to try and say the Our Father instead.
>
> I knelt by the bed and stared at the wall in front of me. I began the Our Father, but I knew I was messing it up because I couldn't remember the words exactly. I knew that if God was really there that He would accept it anyway. I was telling Him in my heart that I wanted to believe in Him and knew that if He was there He could read my heart.
>
> It was then that I felt a presence in the room with me. I felt a feeling of love. This love was of such depth that I can only tell you that I don't believe that human beings are capable of love like that. I knew suddenly that God was there. He wanted me to know that He does indeed exist, that He knew me by name, and that He loved me deeply. That's all. I don't know how long it took, only a minute or less, I think. But it changed my life.

Carol Samuelson discovered a simple truth about prayer that has been around since ancient times: Prayer is essentially "keeping company with God." It begins with the deep inner desire to seek God and it develops into a loving relationship where we give ourselves to God and then respond to God as he makes himself known to us.

"How can you define prayer except by saying that it is love?" suggested Catherine de Hueck Doherty in one of her most popular books on prayer. "It is love expressed in speech, and love expressed in silence. To put it another way, prayer is the meeting of two loves: the love of God and our love. That's all there is to prayer."

As simple as it sounds, many people still wonder if they are doing it the right way or how they can do it better — especially if they have been away from the Church for a while. Perhaps the best way to begin is to simply talk to God from the depths of your heart. Some of the best prayer begins when we admit that we need God and we pour out to God all of our pain, joy, fear, questions, doubts, and anxieties. St. Paul tells us that when we open ourselves to God in this way, what really happens is the Holy Spirit teaches us how to pray by praying with us in the depths of our beings (Romans 8:26-27).

"When we pray, we enter into a process of communicating with God, believing in our deepest being that this communication makes a difference in our lives," suggests Sister Joyce Rupp, OSM.

Good communication between persons always goes both ways — each listens and each responds. So, too, with God and us. Sometimes we speak and sometimes we listen and sometimes there is a lot said without any words coming between the two of us. The wonder of our communion with God is that it can happen anywhere and anytime. Sometimes this event is as simple as seeing the morning star shine upon us and sensing a deep bonding with the magnificent Creator. Other times it is as deliberate as a structured meditation time, or as deep as a moment of intense, intimate silence. And sometimes it is as penetrating as the cry of agony which dwells in a heart full of pain. However it is that we communicate with God, and God with us, the truth is that God is deeply involved in our lives, touching us with love. This touch of God is the touch of transformation. We can never walk closely with God for very long and not have this presence make a difference in our lives, although we may not feel or see that difference for a long time.

One of the biggest pitfalls for people is thinking there is a special feeling we should have when we pray. Sometimes, when we pray, we do experience a sense of deep peace, but it doesn't always happen. "True prayer, pure prayer is in the will to give yourself to God," explains Father John Catoir.

When you put yourself in the presence of the Lord in your own home or at church or anyplace, the only thing you have to do is tell the Lord you want to give yourself to him. You may be having an allergy attack. Your head may be stopped up. The room may be cold. You may be thoroughly conscious of the uncomfortable feelings that you're having, but your prayer is not successful or unsuccessful according to whether or not you feel good about it or whether or not you have been able to concentrate perfectly. Your prayer is valid in and of itself by virtue of the fact that you sincerely want to give yourself to God just as you are — headache and all. All prayer is successful if it is a sincere attempt to give yourself to God. You do not have to force feelings of any kind.

Some people worry about distractions, but Father David LiPuma suggests that distractions may be exactly what you need to pray about. "Maybe God is speaking to you through that distraction."

Father Catoir warns that if you're overly concerned about distractions, maybe you're being too hard on yourself. "If you go into church, you go with the intention of giving yourself to God," he explains. "No sooner do you sit down, and the distractions start: *I have to do this. I have to do that. I have to call so and so.* The Lord is the last thing you're thinking about. After 15 minutes you say to yourself, 'This is ridiculous. This never works.' Then you leave and you say to yourself, 'I have failed again.' But by putting yourself down, you have ignored the importance of what you did and the purity of your intention, which was to give yourself to God."

Sometimes people worry about what form their prayer should take. Part of the beauty of Catholicism is that there are many different styles of spirituality — Jesuit, Franciscan, Benedictine, Carmelite, Eastern, Charismatic — and many different ways of expressing our prayer. We can pray out loud or silently. We can pray by singing, by whispering, or by speaking in tongues. We can kneel, sit, dance or lie prostrate. We can pray alone or with others. We can pray in a way that is spontaneous or we can use formal prayers. We can participate in the celebration of the Eucharist, which is the highest and most perfect form of prayer. We can pray by reading Scripture. We can meditate. We can keep a spiritual journal in which we write our prayers. We can read spiritual books. We can pray with icons or religious objects. We can volunteer in a soup kitchen or a homeless shelter. We can go on a pilgrimage to a holy place. We can have our own special devotions, like the Stations of the Cross, or novenas, or prayers to the Blessed Mother and the saints. We can go on a retreat. We can pray by talking to God, thinking about God, or simply by placing ourselves silently in the presence of God. We can make every moment of our day a prayer by offering all that we are and all that we do to God.

Thousands of books have been written on various forms of prayer, but you will have to decide for yourself what style of prayer is right for you. You might hear from certain people that you should read Scripture, or say the Rosary, or pray to St. Jude, or visit the Blessed Sacrament. St. Ignatius Loyola would disagree. He warned that there is "no greater mistake in spiritual matters than to force others to follow one's own pattern."

One young woman who came back to the Catholic Church after making the rounds of Protestant and non-denominational congregations agrees:

"Concentrate on your own relationship with Jesus, and not so much on what other people around you are doing or thinking. As trite as this may sound, I firmly believe

that God really wants a 'relationship' with his people."
Stephanie Roy

Depending on your background, your temperament, and your personality, there will be some types of prayer that appeal to you more than others.

Frank Barbarossa, M.D., of Amherst, New York, came back to the Church through Scripture:

> "Scripture changed my life. It helped me appreciate more and more the relationship between God and myself and other people. It makes me a better Catholic because now I can appreciate the Eucharist as a real event rather than a ritual."

For Gary and Ginnie Ingold of Clarence, New York, a devotion to Our Lady is an essential element in their prayer life:

> "You can get straight to Jesus. We have always believed that. But the Blessed Mother purifies everything we do and she takes everything perfectly to her Son."

Frank Johnston of Cumming, Georgia, prefers to commune with God in silence:

> "I learned to treat the Lord as a beloved friend. I spend time with Him. I don't have to say anything or recite prayers. I just relax and enjoy His company. Sometimes He speaks to me, often in the most subtle ways."

An intellectual might prefer structured prayer or discursive meditation. Creative people might lean toward using their imagination in prayer by placing themselves in a Scripture passage. Someone else might prefer the traditional methods of prayer they remember from their childhood.

"Pray as you can," advised Abbot John Chapman, who

headed a Benedictine monastery in England during the early part of the twentieth century. "Don't try to pray as you cannot."

Father Gary Bagley agrees: "I don't think prayer is trying to find the secret code for the inscrutable God as much as it is believing that you're not alone in this. If you want the ultimate prayer, look at Jesus during the agony in the garden when he prayed, 'Not my will, but thine be done.'"

Chapter Notes

"... keeping company with God": *Handbook for Today's Catholic*, A Redemptorist Pastoral Publication, Liguori Publications, 1991, p. 61.

"How can you define prayer except by saying that it is love?": Catherine de Hueck Doherty, *Soul of My Soul*, Notre Dame: Ave Maria Press, 1985, p. 8.

"When we pray...": Rupp, *Praying our Good-byes*, pp. 78-79.

CHAPTER 9

Thy Will Be Done

"I have considered returning to the Catholic Church, but I would only do this if I was convinced that this was God's leading and voice." *Angelo Natalie, Connecticut*

"In order to return to the Catholic Church I would have to divorce my husband or tell him we had to live as brother and sister, which would probably result in his leaving me anyway. Is this what God wants?" *M.D., New York*

"I'm trying to figure out God's will in my life, but I need some help. What signals does God give to guide a person to his will? How does one know those signals are from God and not subconscious wishful thinking?" *T.L.*

The process of figuring out God's will is always a major concern of people who are trying to decide whether or not to come back to the Catholic Church. Some people want to know if God has some special purpose or plan for their lives. Others wonder if God may have spoken to them through something someone said, or through an uncanny event, or through a Scripture passage, or during an intense moment of prayer.

"A lot of people today are searching for something deeper in their lives," says Father David LiPuma, who conducts special workshops on discernment for alienated Catholics. "They begin to search for God, and they want to know how they'll be able to tell if God is speaking to them."

"I know that prayer is the focal point in learning God's will, but sometimes I think either God's being quiet or I'm not listening very well." *L.T.*

Father LiPuma believes that God does speak to us, but not in a voice that we hear audibly. Instead, the Holy Spirit speaks to us through ideas, inspirations, longings, and deep desires of the heart. You can be sure this kind of prompting comes from God if it urges you to do what is good. God never leads us toward what is sinful or wrong.

"God nudges people all the time," Father LiPuma says, but unless you are paying attention, you might not realize it is God.

When we become more in tune with our spirituality, we begin to notice that a chance meeting with someone, or a fleeting thought about someone, or something out of the ordinary might be God speaking to me in this moment. Maybe it's God's way of saying, "You need to call that person," or "You need to think about this," or "You need to wake up and make some changes in your daily routine."
It isn't always a warm, fuzzy feeling. Sometimes in those dark moments God keeps whispering, "I am very near," but because we are so absorbed in our pain, we don't hear him.
Sometimes we try to run away from the painful things in our lives, but maybe what God is asking us to do is to face them. If we find ourselves avoiding something, we should stop and ask ourselves what is really going on. Why are we trying to run away?
When people say they want to learn how to recognize God's voice in their lives, I suggest saying this simple prayer every morning: "Lord, whatever happens this day, please guide me and show me the way." Once you begin to realize that God is constantly speaking

to you, your life takes on a different spiritual dimension. God becomes real. You begin to see God working in your life and in the lives of other people.

As people become aware of God's presence, they sometimes begin to wonder if God is asking them to do something specific. For example:

- Does God want me to stay in this marriage or to separate from my abusive spouse?
- Does God want me to come back to the Catholic Church or stay in the Lutheran Church where we were married and raised our children?
- Does God want me to leave this job and start a new career where I can lead a simpler life and help other people?
- Does God want me to file for an annulment?
- Does God want me to stop using birth control even though my doctor told me that another pregnancy could kill me?
- Does God want me to break off my engagement because there is no hope of ever getting an annulment and being married in the Church?

Sometimes the answer is painfully obvious. We know in the depths of ourselves exactly what it is that God wants. But sometimes God's will is not very clear. When we face a difficult conflict involving our spiritual life or our relationship with God, the process of decision-making takes on a different dimension, which is called discernment because it involves prayer, reflection, and listening to the Holy Spirit. The steps include:

- Asking for spiritual insight, wisdom, and understanding.
- Searching the Scriptures for guidance.
- Consulting the teaching of the Church.
- Seeking the advice of a priest or other experts.

- Discussing the situation with people who will be affected.
- Recognizing your own feelings.
- Sorting out the details of the situation.
- Making a list of options and possible consequences.
- Weighing the alternatives in your own conscience.
- Listening to the movement of the Holy Spirit in your soul.

These steps are not always as simple as they appear. You might wish that God would say, "Do this" or "Don't do that." Some people point out that God does give definite do's and don'ts in the Ten Commandments and through the teachings of the Church. The problem, however, is that life situations can fall into gray areas where the distinctions between right and wrong are sometimes blurred. Sometimes it is simply not clear what it is that God really wants you to do.

> "I told Jesus, 'If you are really there, and if you are really calling me to this thing of conversion, which I'm beginning to doubt, then I'll make one more phone call. But this is all very embarrassing so just one more call, Okay?'
> The next call was to a parish where someone said, 'Let's get together. How about tomorrow?'
> My advice to anyone in this situation is to keep searching as long as you can to find your way back, but if you really feel too humiliated and hung out by your shyness, throw it on the Lord. If he is truly calling you, and you are truly answering the call, he won't let go of you. He'll never let you down." *Jo Cunningham, California*

It is sometimes conceivable that situations arise where God has no preference for what you do. For example, suppose you sense that God is drawing you back to the Church. Does God have a preference as to whether you join a parish with traditional styles of worship or a parish with an emphasis on social justice? It is probably safe to say that in this case God wants you to go where you will feel spiritually nourished. "Being in tune with your heart is part of discernment," says Father Bob Hughes.

In *Thoughts in Solitude*, Thomas Merton wrote: "My Lord God, I have no idea where I am going. I do not see the road ahead of me. I cannot know for certain where it will end. Nor do I really know myself, and the fact that I think that I am following your will does not mean that I am actually doing so. But I believe that the desire to please you does in fact please you. And I hope I have that desire in all that I am doing. I hope that I will never do anything apart from that desire. And I know that if I do this you will lead me by the right road though I may know nothing about it."

Bishop Fulton J. Sheen suggested that God sometimes speaks to us through our subconscious mind: "God can guide us quite naturally in a particular direction without our being aware of it. What was it, for example, that induced Paul Claudel, an agnostic and unbeliever, to enter Notre Dame Cathedral at midnight on Christmas, and ultimately to receive the gift of faith? Here was a reasonable man who was guided unreasonably. Very often stupid people come to God through very reasonable arguments, and reasonable people come to God through no arguments at all."

God pursues us constantly with the hope of drawing us to himself, but it is always a very subtle movement within the soul, and we are always free to say "yes" or "no" to the gentle invitations. God never forces us to do anything, but he never stops nudging us, either.

Sometimes, when we sense that God is pursuing us, we become fearful and try to run away. The mystic poet, Francis Thompson, described the Divine pursuit of a soul in his classic poem, "The Hound of Heaven," which paints in word pictures the image of a soul trying to escape from God by fleeing to other people, the things of this world, nature, the love of children. When all hope of escape is exhausted, the soul hears God's voice saying, "Everything failed you because you fled from me." God stretches out his hand with another invitation to come, and the soul finally finds love and happiness in God's embrace.

"I am beginning now to see how radically the character of my spiritual journey will change when I no longer think of God as hiding out and making it difficult as possible for me to find him, but, instead, as the one who is looking for me while I am doing the hiding," wrote Father Henri Nouwen. "When I look through God's eyes at my innermost self and discover God's joy at my coming home, then my life may become less anguished and more trusting."

Perhaps the real answer to the question of what God wants is that God wants us to respond to his love. As St. Augustine wrote: "Love God, and do what you will."

Only you can decide what that means in your life. "One moves out of the realm of rights, law, civic equality, as soon as one is governed by love," wrote Bishop Sheen. "It changes not only ourselves; it changes others."

> "My husband didn't want to go to church, so I catered to his desires. I realize now what a mistake I made. At the time I thought I was doing the right thing by catering to my husband. Now I go to church every Sunday and I feel much happier and stronger in my relationship to God and to other people." *Annie Dutt*

Chapter Notes

"My Lord God...": Thomas Merton, *Thoughts in Solitude*, New York: Farrar, Straus and Giroux, 1986, p. 83.

"God can guide us quite naturally...": Fulton J. Sheen, *From the Angel's Blackboard: The Best of Fulton J. Sheen*, Liguori, Missouri: Triumph Books, 1995, pp. 23-24.

"I am beginning now to see...": Henri J. Nouwen, *The Return of the Prodigal Son*, New York: Doubleday, 1992, p. 101.

"One moves out of the realm of rights...": Fulton J. Sheen, *From the Angel's Blackboard*, p. 148.

CHAPTER 10

Changes in the Church Since Vatican II

"After 24 years, I returned. I must say that things sure were different from what I remembered! What was this? Catholics singing??? Holding hands???" *Gene Kinnaly, Jacksonville, Florida*

"As an altar boy, I was taught that the host was the Body of Christ and no one was to touch it except the priest. Now it is handed to people. This seems totally against what the Church taught me. The change has caused me to no longer see the Catholic Church as I once did." *B.N.*

"The Mass is confusing to me. I'm usually not on the right page at the right time, even though our church secretary sat down with me and explained the ins and outs of it. The Church 'lingo' is still a mystery. I wish there was a Catholic Dictionary!" *Janice Haber, Guthrie, Oklahoma.*

In the days before Vatican II, everything seemed clear. Catholics went to Confession on Saturday and Mass on Sunday. Women covered their heads in church. Everyone genuflected. The tabernacle was in the center of the church. There were High Masses and Low Masses, Benediction, Forty Hours, Stations of the Cross, May crownings and Corpus Christi processions. Nuns wore habits. Unbaptized babies went to limbo. Only

Catholics went to heaven. And in response to the invocation: "Savior of the World," the congregation replied, "Save Russia."

On January 25, 1959, Pope John XXIII stunned the College of Cardinals by calling for an ecumenical council. The Council opened on October 11, 1962, and during the next three years, produced sixteen documents that revolutionized the Catholic Church. The major changes affected how Catholics worshipped, the role of lay people in the Church, their relationship with non-Catholics, their access to Scripture, and how they should live out the Gospel spirit of love toward God, neighbor and self. These changes left some people in a state of shock.

> "I feel as if the Church left me. I grew up attending Mass every Sunday, Holy Day and first Friday. I felt a certain camaraderie with all other Catholics world-wide. We learned what the Latin translation of the liturgy was in English and could attend a Mass in not just another diocese, but in any other country and still feel at home. The Church that I now occasionally attend was evidently designed by a child of the sixties or seventies. It appears to be a collaboration of Frank Lloyd Wright and Picasso. Sometimes the incense or the smell of the snuffed out candles brings back some of the unquestioning faith of my youth, but there are no recognizable physical remnants in the sights and sounds. It is difficult to feel at home."
> *Vince Lyons*

Changes in prayer and worship had the most immediate impact on people in the pews. Church custodians installed new altars in front of the old ones, uprooted communion rails, wired the sanctuaries for microphones, and moved the tabernacle off the main altar. During Mass, the priest faced the people, and instead of mumbling in Latin, he read aloud in English, making the quality of his performance a new area for commentary and criticism. Catholics who had been trained to pray silently and privately during the Latin Mass, now had words to say, songs to sing, and hands to shake.

"I went to Catholic school for 12 years, but fell away when all the nuns left the convent to get married and the priests took away Latin and introduced bizarre practices like baptizing babies during the Mass." *S.M.*

Change is hard for some people, and what made it even harder was the way some priests ridiculed the old ways by scolding people for kneeling instead of standing to receive Communion or for fingering a Rosary during Mass. Lay people became Eucharistic ministers and lectors, which spawned a whole new kind of gossip: *"He only does it to create visibility for himself and his business... She was out partying last night and this morning she's handing out Holy Communion!"* During these chaotic times, rumors also spread that "liberated" priests in casual clothes were consecrating pancakes and grape juice or pizza and beer in private homes. Sometimes, unfortunately, those rumors were true.

Anne Roche Muggeridge believes many Catholics experienced "a sudden, desolating feeling that there is no longer Anybody there, a moment of panic as the stomach reacts before the reason kicks in."

"It happened to my father and he left the Church," she writes.

It happened to me years ago, at a late afternoon Mass in a church I used to attend. There were only a few people in the church. The young priest behaved in a particularly wild and frivolous manner (he was, as it turned out, just about to leave the priesthood under unsavory circumstances)... Halfway through the Mass, I went out and sat on a wall outside the church and wept in rage, panic, and despair. I sat there a long time and then I went home.

"A lot of abuses took place in liturgies because the priests weren't formed in liturgical theology," admits Msgr. Angelo Caligiuri, who worked in Rome during the Vatican Council and understood the reasoning behind the liturgical reforms. "When I was trained to say Mass, if I moved my hands beyond my shoulders, I was committing a sin. When we came out of that rigid structure, it was difficult — especially for some of the young priests who didn't have a good grounding in the old and didn't have the time to come to a mature understanding of the new."

What people in the pews experienced was a drastic upheaval in the external practices of the liturgy without any real understanding of why the changes were made. To many, it felt as if someone had stripped away all that was sacred and holy.

Even the language changed and a whole new Catholic jargon came into use:

- The Mass also became known as Liturgy or the Eucharist or the Table of the Lord, or the Eucharistic Celebration.

- Sermons were replaced by homilies, which meant that instead of just preaching on any topic, the subject matter focused on the readings of the Mass.

- The Priest at Mass became the Celebrant or Presider.

- Baptism, First Communion, and Confirmation were grouped together as the Sacraments of Initiation.

- Convert classes became the Rite of Christian Initiation for Adults or RCIA.

- Someone who tried to live their faith was called "a Witness." When they talked about their faith (which Catholics rarely did before Vatican II), it was called "witnessing" or giving a "witness talk."

- Charismatic Renewal emerged as a Catholic Pentecostal prayer movement that focused on devotion to the Holy Spirit and included phenomena such as baptism in the Spirit, speaking in tongues and being slain in the Spirit.

- Catholic Action or Apostolates became known as Ministries, and lay people with the title "pastoral minister," took over some of the work formerly done by nuns and priests.

- Eucharistic Ministers distributed Communion at Masses and to the sick at home and in hospitals.

- Music Ministers and cantors lead everyone in singing.

- Lectors read the Scripture passages and announcements at Mass.

- Deacons appeared in parishes, but no one was quite sure what they were supposed to do.

- Liturgical dance emerged as a form of prayer.

- CCD became Religious Education, and someone called a DRE or Director of Religious Education made the rules.

- Holy Hours and Forty Hours Devotions became Eucharistic Adoration.

- Confession became the Sacrament of Reconciliation, and people were urged to talk to the priest face-to-face in a Reconciliation Room.

- Sacramental preparation emerged as the term for required classes on Baptism, first Reconciliation, first Communion, Confirmation, and Marriage.

- Extreme Unction or Last Rites became the Sacrament of the Sick.

Thirty years later, most Catholics say they like the changes in the Church. A whopping 77% say they don't mind shaking hands at the sign of peace; 73% approve of Eucharistic Ministers; 77% like altar girls; 76% like the homilies they hear; but only 44% think baptisms should take place during Sunday Mass. Communion services led by non-ordained ministers find approval with only 29% of Catholics, and only 14% like liturgical dance. Over half say they participate in some parish function, while 35% read the Bible at least once a month, and 63% discuss religious issues with others at least once a month.

"I left the Church before Vatican II, and returned after all
the changes. Culture shock! But what love and peace I
found when I came back." *Elizabeth Feetters, Ravenna, Ohio*

Most people who come back to the Church like the new
focus on love instead of the fear, sin, and legalism that domi-
nated the pre-Vatican II Church. In the old days, Catholics went
to Confession often, but never felt as if they were worthy enough
to go to Communion. They feared the punishments God would
inflict on them for not being perfect. The attitude emerged that
nuns and priests, who lived under vows of poverty, chastity and
obedience were somehow better than ordinary people who en-
gaged in pleasures of the flesh. Among religious, the cloistered
ones, who left the world for a life of prayer, were considered
the holiest of all.

This unwarranted emphasis on sin negated the true Catholic belief in God's unconditional love, mercy and forgiveness.
One of the major accomplishments of the Second Vatican Council was to reinforce the truth that all of God's creation is good.
It freed Catholics to live lives of love and service for God and
each other with the assurance that in spite of human weaknesses, God will never stop loving them. Most people like that
new emphasis.

"I feel as if I have been released from the bondage of fear
and punishment that was hammered into me in Catholic
elementary and high school." *B.O.*

Still, there are a good number of Catholics who miss
Gregorian chant, incense, the mysterious movements and the
pageantry that impacted their senses and carried them into a
more mystical state of prayer. For some, the Latin Mass was a
time for personal meditation that could never be replaced. Lit-
urgists insist that those personal practices grew because no one
understood the Latin words of the Mass. The premise behind
the use of the vernacular was to bring people into fuller par-

ticipation in the Mass by going back to the prayers and practices of the early Christians.

Recognizing that the drastic weaning from the old was too
difficult for many Catholics, Pope John Paul II authorized cel-
ebrations of the Latin Mass with the permission of local bishops. Today, many parishes are resurrecting some of the old
music and devotions. It's not unusual to find people gathering
to say the Rosary after daily Mass. Some parishes have reintro-
duced Eucharistic Adoration, Stations of the Cross and Benediction.

> "I found a church in my community that was 'traditional'
> by calling the Catholic bookstore and simply asking. I also
> found out that if I so desired I could attend a Mass in
> Latin." *Kim von Aspern*

Changes in other sacraments after Vatican II also occurred
in an attempt to bring them closer to their original meaning and
purpose. Take Baptism, for example.

> "I had a baby out of wedlock. When I wanted to have her
> baptized, the priest told me 'no.' He said I would obvi-
> ously 'not raise her to be a good Catholic.' My father
> baptized her in the kitchen sink because he was afraid that
> she wouldn't go to heaven if she died." *M.F.*

Before the Second Vatican Council, priests baptized babies
as soon as possible because the Church emphasized the need
for a soul to be cleansed of original sin. After the Vatican Council, the emphasis on Baptism changed to the early Christian
understanding of the sacrament as a Rite of Initiation into the
community of the Church. Because of the change in emphasis,
the rules changed, too.

"Canonically, baptism is offered to those parents about
whom we have a founded hope that they will bring the child
up in the faith," explains Msgr. William Gallagher.

What does "founded hope" mean? Some priests take the law very literally and say, "You have to go to church for 6 months before I do this baptism." Others take a broader interpretation and assume that the parents came to the church because they recognize their responsibility toward raising the child Catholic.

When we baptize a child, the baptismal rite says, "You are the first teachers of your child in the ways of the faith. Be good teachers by practicing the faith and teaching your child to do so by keeping the Commandments." So it really is your responsibility.

If you come to me and say, "Look, I'm a Catholic, and I want my child to be Catholic. I haven't been around lately because I'm pregnant, and my husband is working two jobs, and we just moved." Well, those are real things and I'll take your word for it. Why? Because it's *your* responsibility.

When people have fights over this with other priests, I tell them, "Look. Don't get mad at the priest. He's doing exactly what he's been trained to do. Call the Chancery and find another priest who is going to help you. It's good for your child to be raised in the faith, so after the baby is baptized, register in a parish and raise that baby to be a good Catholic."

Similar changes occurred with wedding ceremonies. Gone are the days when a priest would conduct a quick ceremony for a pregnant bride. The rising divorce rate and the Church's teaching that marriage is a permanent union has created a climate of extreme caution. Today, marriage preparation classes are usually required, and a priest can delay or even refuse the sacrament if he believes that there is some impediment to a valid exchange of consent between both parties.

With the new attitude toward ecumenism, dispensations are now granted for Catholics to be married in non-Catholic ceremonies, sometimes with a priest and a minister or rabbi present. Non-Catholics are no longer forced to sign a statement saying they will raise the children Catholic, but Catholics in an interfaith marriage are still urged to raise the children Catholic.

Most of the anti-Protestant attitudes in the pre-Vatican II Church came from the teachings of the Council of Trent (1545-63), which were a defensive reaction to the Reformation. For example, before Vatican II, Catholics emphasized that sacraments produced grace. That emphasis came in reaction to John Calvin, who held that the Catholic teaching on the sacraments was akin to magic. Today the Catholic Church teaches that a sacrament is a personal encounter with Jesus Christ. Grace is still part of the sacrament, but it is no longer the main emphasis.

Likewise, as Protestant reformers attacked the hierarchy of the Church, Catholics responded by emphasizing the authority of the hierarchy. "Everything got stamped with Church authority, from the serious (It's a mortal sin to miss Mass on Sunday) to the trivial (It's a mortal sin to eat a hot dog on Friday) because all were leveled by one measurement: contempt for Church authority," writes Father William J. Bausch in his handbook for returning Catholics.

In the same context, Scripture reading was not emphasized in the pre-Vatican II Church because Martin Luther claimed that Scripture alone was the source of faith. The Catholic Church reacted by emphasizing Tradition, and we were told to leave the interpretation of Scripture to the Church.

> "I have been away from the Church for 35 years. I heard that confession changed after Vatican II. Aside from going face-to-face, what else is different?" *T.R.*

Since Vatican II the new sacramental rite of Penance is called Reconciliation. While the new rite encourages face-to-face confession because it is more personal and better suited for personal healing, you can still choose the privacy of the confessional screen. The reason for the change was to move away from the old grocery list of sins that people used to rattle off weekly, and to encourage people to use the sacrament for deeper spiritual healing and an on-going conversion that helps shape our lives more closely to the life and teachings of Jesus Christ.

The Church now emphasizes that each individual sin has consequences for the whole community. Sometimes, especially during Lent and Advent, a parish will have a communal penance service with prayers, Scripture readings, and music, followed by the opportunity for individual confession. In this way, the people in the parish restore their relationship with God and with the community. Parish bulletins usually list the times when priests are in the confessionals or reconciliation rooms. You also have the option of making a private appointment with a priest.

The age and sequence of First Communion and Confirmation also changed after Vatican II with some dioceses choosing to confirm before a child receives First Communion and other dioceses moving Confirmation back to high school years. The lack of conformity creates problems for families who are transferred frequently.

"I never made my Confirmation because we moved a lot, and my parents finally gave up on trying to figure out the Church rules. They told us we could decide ourselves if we wanted to be confirmed when we were in college."
C.L.

Another sacrament that underwent a radical change was Extreme Unction, which used to be the final anointing of a dying person, but is now called the Sacrament of the Sick, and can be administered to anyone suffering from serious physical, mental, or emotional illnesses.

"When my father died, my brother called to see if a priest could come. The person he spoke to said priests don't do that anymore. A Protestant minister and his wife live next door, so my mom sent my brother over to get him because she didn't want my father to leave the house without being prayed over. The reverend came over and said a nice prayer." *P.E., Rochester, New York*

The change in emphasis from Last Rites to Sacrament of the Sick has caused tremendous pain and misunderstanding. Priests still anoint dying people, but the Church now teaches that the Sacrament of the Sick can be administered days or even weeks before someone dies. Many parishes offer the Sacrament of the Sick during special healing Masses for the elderly, for people who are seriously ill, for those scheduled for serious surgery, and for people suffering from addictions, mental illness, anxiety and despair.

Another major change took place in the liturgy for funerals. The name was changed from the Mass of the Dead with the priest wearing black to the Mass of Christian Burial with the priest dressed in white to emphasize the power of Christ's resurrection. During the funeral Mass, the casket is covered with a white pall that represents the white garments that the person wore during Baptism.

You might remember the old days when people who were divorced, people who committed suicide, and people who had drifted away from the Church or didn't use their envelopes on Sundays were denied a Catholic funeral. After Vatican II, these restrictions on funerals were lifted. Today, most priests see funerals as a moment of grace for the family, yet stories of priests denying Christian burial still abound. Sometimes it is a misunderstanding. Sometimes the priest is wrong. In any case, if someone in your family is denied a Catholic funeral or if the circumstances don't seem right, it is wise to call the Chancery for clarification.

"When my father died on Palm Sunday, the pastor told the undertaker that we'd have to keep the body in storage until the day after Easter as it was totally impossible to have any sort of burial service whatsoever during Holy

Week. Well, my brother called the chancellor of the archdiocese, who said, 'That's a load of… You can't have a funeral Eucharist, but you can have a burial office!'" *Mary E. O'Shaughnessy, New York*

"There is a lot of pain out there," admits Msgr. Gallagher. "We caused some of it and some of it was caused by the changes in the Church. Sometimes people cause their own pain, but it seems to me that it's the responsibility of the Church to minister to everyone in a way that is kind and understanding. The problem is that we're all human."

Chapter Notes

"a sudden desolating feeling…": Anne Roche Muggeridge, *The Desolate City: Revolution in the Catholic Church*, San Francisco: Harper & Row, 1990, p. 134.

"It happened to my father…": *Ibid.*

Thirty years later, most Catholics say…: Thomas P. Sweetser, SJ, "The Parish: What Has Changed, What Remains?" *America*, February 17, 1996, pp. 6-7.

"Everything got stamped with Church authority…": William J. Bausch, *While You Were Gone: A Handbook for Returning Catholics*, Mystic, Connecticut: Twenty-Third Publications, 1994, p. 61.

CHAPTER 11

The Human Side of the Church

"Looking back upon the history of the Church, I see great violence and misery brought upon others in the name of God." *C. Bruce Santore II, Reynoldsburg, Ohio*

"I have an uncle who became a deacon in the Church. Along with becoming a deacon, he became the biggest pompous ass I have ever known and he has deeply hurt my mother in the process." *E.C., Kentucky*

"I question the Church's commitment to peace and to helping the homeless. We have a homeless population here, but what my parish found important was raising over $100,000 to buy a glass crucifix! What are our priorities?" *Kevin McHugh, Andover, Kansas*

"The priest gave two sermons on Palm Sunday scolding parents on their kids' behavior. On Easter Sunday, the priest tried to humiliate the standing-room-only crowd. I need this in my life like I need another bill." *R.D.*

During the early part of this century, a group of soap box orators called the Catholic Evidence Guild spoke on London street corners and squares. "Our lectures usually took around fifteen minutes, in the rest of the hour the crowd questioned us," recalled Frank Sheed. "Upon the papacy and the Church history generally we had week after week, year after year, as unsparing a *viva voce* examination as has been known in the world — every charge ever brought against a Pope was leered at us, sneered at us."

Hecklers pointed out that there were popes who bought the papacy, popes who stole the papacy, and for a number of years there were two, and then three popes all claiming the papal crown. Pope John XII (955-963) was stabbed to death by a jealous husband who found the Pope in bed with his wife. Pope Alexander VI (1492-1503) fathered a brood of illegitimate children. Pope Stephen VII (896-897) dug up the body of his predecessor, dressed the corpse in pontifical robes for a false trial, and found him guilty of becoming pope under false pretenses.

The Catholic Evidence Guild speakers knew that they weren't there to defend the sins of the popes, however. Their purpose was to introduce people to the Catholic Church.

"We had to show them the Church Christ founded exactly as it was and is," Sheed recalled. "If they were scandalized by what they saw, they must take it up with Christ, who founded it, or with the Holy Spirit, who vivifies it... Our aim was to show why we, knowing the worst — knowing indeed a worse worst than they themselves knew — still knew ourselves in union with Christ. However ill he might be served by his representative at any time, we could still find in his Church, as nowhere else, life and truth and the possibility of union with him to the limit of our willingness."

There's an old saying that the Catholic Church is 99.9% human and only .1% divine, but that .1% is all that's needed. "What that means is there is a human element in the Church that is going to make mistakes," says Father Tom Doyle, "but the other side of that equation is God working through human weakness. You have to balance it out."

Perhaps looking back at some of the human elements in Church history will help put all of this into perspective. If you start at the beginning, you see that Jesus chose as the head of the Church a man who questioned, doubted, didn't understand, and denied him three times. But Jesus also promised that the Holy Spirit would be with the Church until the end of time and the gates of hell would not prevail against it. After Pentecost, it was the power of the Holy Spirit that transformed Peter into a fearless preacher and leader. That didn't mean that Peter or the early Christians didn't continue to struggle. If you read the Acts of the Apostles, you will see that there were divisions in the Church right from the start over how much of the Jewish law the Gentile converts had to observe.

"It is well to remind ourselves of St. Paul," suggests C.G. Jung, "and his split consciousness: on one side he felt he was the apostle directly called and enlightened by God, and, on the other hand, a sinful man who could not pluck out the 'thorn in the flesh' and rid himself of the Satanic angel who plagued him. That is to say, even the most enlightened person remains what he is, and is never more than his own limited ego before the One who dwells within him, whose form has no knowable boundaries, who encompasses him on all sides, fathomless as the abysms of the earth and vast as the sky."

It was humanness in the Church that roused controversies through the ages as people tried to understand and adapt Christian principles to their lives and times, while still remaining true to the Scriptures and Tradition. Early Christians, for instance, never depicted Jesus on a cross because in their society the cross was a scandal. By the fifth century, you'll find a bare cross with a lamb next to it. With only two known exceptions, the body of Christ did not appear on the cross until the end of the sixth century, and in those instances Jesus wore a long tunic. When a Greek representation of Jesus suffering on the cross appeared in the tenth century, Rome condemned it as blasphemy, and yet today, you see crucifixes in Catholic homes and churches all over the world.

These kinds of minor disagreements seem like nothing

when compared to the involvement of churchmen in the massive killing of innocent people during the Crusades, the persecution of Jews, the tortures of the Spanish Inquisition, or the burning of heretics at the stake. Yet throughout the darkest moments of Church history, God has inspired other men and women to serve as models of goodness and holiness.

- In the early 13th century, St. Francis of Assisi and his band of itinerant preachers lived in voluntary poverty while the Imperial papacy was preoccupied with wealth and power.

- In the 14th century, when divisions between French and Italian cardinals produced two popes vying for power, St. Bridget of Sweden and St. Catherine of Siena both worked for ecclesiastical reform and Church unity.

- During the Spanish Inquisition, St. Teresa of Avila and St. John of the Cross overcame hostile opposition from powerful Church officials and succeeded in reforming the religious life of the Carmelites in Spain.

- In the early 20th century, when rationalism and war shook people to their roots, St. Therese of Lisieux inspired millions through her "little way" of finding God through small actions in day to day life.

"As I have told hundreds of audiences, the holiness of the Church is not the sum total of the holiness of all who belong to her, any more than the wetness of the rain is measured by the wetness of all who have gone out into it," insists Frank Sheed.

> If millions get wet, the rain is no wetter: if everyone stays indoors, the rain is no less wet. The Church is holy because it is Christ living on in the world. Its holiness therefore is a constant, neither increased nor diminished by our response... The saints have responded totally, they have exposed themselves to the force of the rain, so to speak, and in their countless thousands they stand

as proof to you and me that in the Church holiness is to
be had for the willing. In regard to every saint we can
say — there, but for resistance to the grace of God, go I.

For many people, recognizing and accepting the difference
between the human and the divine paves the way for returning to Catholicism.

"I looked all over and I have not found a Church yet that
doesn't have lots of negative areas now or in its history.
Some things never change. I might as well be Catholic."
T.I.

There are others, however, who have a harder time accepting the human versus divine argument.

"One of the biggest dual messages sent out is putting
brothers, nuns, and priests on a pedestal but then if
something is done by the person, we are told, 'They are
only human.'" *Eilish Maura*

Yet, the reality is that there is a human side of the Church.
"And it is some kind of miracle, surely, that a community so
passionately attacked from without and so humiliatingly cor-
rupt and rent with factions within has managed to survive for
two millennia," says Father William J. O'Malley, SJ.

In November, 1994, Pope John Paul II called for the entire
Church to make an examination of conscience and to openly
confess and make reparation for the past errors, inconsistencies,
and atrocities committed in the Church's name during the past
1000 years. "Acknowledging the weakness of the past is an act
of honesty and courage which helps us strengthen our faith,
which alerts us to face today's temptations and challenges and
prepares us to meet them," the Pope wrote.

John Paul II has already revoked the condemnation of
Galileo, who was found guilty by the Inquisition in June 1633
for insisting that the earth revolved around the sun.

During a trip to Africa the Pope apologized for the involvement of churchmen in the slave trade. In Morocco he deplored the excesses of the Crusades. In Santo Domingo, he acknowledged the injustices of churchmen toward the natives of the Americas, and in a Rome synagogue, he spoke against the injustices toward Jews and the errors of the Inquisition.

"Yes, there have been atrocities throughout Church history," insists Jesuit historian Father James Hennesey. "At the same time, there has always been sanctity in the Church. But I don't think most people leave the Catholic Church because they are shocked at what Pope Alexander VI did. Most people struggle over problems they perceive within the Church as they experience it during their own lifetime."

> "I was brought up in the 1950's to believe the Catholic Church was superior. After many years of trying to be a perfect Catholic, I finally gave up and joined a Protestant Church. I never found being Catholic comforting. Frankly, I felt the Catholic Church was judgmental, small-minded, exclusive, and at times, physically and psychologically abusive." *R.T.*

To understand why some American Catholics experienced a Church that seemed negative and narrow, it helps to look at the history, the culture and the mentality of the times. Just as the Council of Trent (1545-63) was a defensive reaction against the attacks of Protestant Reformers, many of the rules and practices of the Catholic Church in America developed as a defensive reaction against the attacks of American Protestants.

In the late 1700's, when the United States was forming, Catholics numbered only 35,000 out of a population of 4 million. As waves of Catholic immigrants arrived in the 1800's, some Protestant groups feared that Catholicism would unravel the fabric of American society, and they unleashed a torrent of anti-Catholic prejudices that filtered into public schools where

Protestant values were reinforced with Protestant prayers and Scripture readings. Textbooks contained inflammatory anti-Catholic interpretations of history. The dunce hat was a mockery of a bishop's miter.

Catholics saw this as a conspiracy to wipe out their religion and culture, and by 1884, the American bishops decreed that parents should send their children to parish-sponsored Catholic schools. For the next 80 years, Catholics practiced segregation by choice. Some people saw it as a reasonable reaction to the anti-Catholic bias of the day. Others called it a ghetto mentality.

During this time period, the Church also operated in an immigrant culture where the father was the disciplinarian. "Many times, when I was a young priest, I would tell the nuns, 'Don't send the child to me when he does something wrong. That makes me the punisher and it creates a poor relationship between clergy and young children,'" recalls Msgr. Rupert Wright. "But they did it anyway."

Society gave tacit approval to strict discipline. Many nuns and priests came from homes where corporal punishment was used, and some joined religious orders because they wanted to escape poverty or abusive situations. Some nuns, who might have preferred nursing or social work, were forced "under obedience" by their superiors into the classroom. Without much teacher training, many nuns faced large classes, which they controlled through intimidation and fear. No one ever thought about what kind of psychological or emotional impact this might have on a child.

"All these things flowed from a lack of knowledge and the cultural conditions at the time," Msgr. Wright insists. "Vatican II was the major changing point."

> "After all those things the nuns told us about sex, we sat there and watched as they ran away to marry priests. My whole faith system shut down at that point." *P.McM.*

There is no accurate method of validating the actual numbers of nuns and priests who left in the 1960's and 70's. It is fair to say that as difficult as it was for the lay people to witness this mass exodus, it was not easy for the men and women who were seeking dispensations from their vows either.

"I remember a priest friend of mine," recalls Msgr. William Stanton. "After Vatican II he began to question the divinity of Christ. He left the priesthood and lost his faith. He became an agnostic. He eventually married, and his wife asked me one time why I was never affected by this. I told her that he always held the institution of the Church on a pedestal, and after Vatican II it all collapsed for him."

For many fallen-away Catholics, the greatest struggle revolves around the sometimes vicious in-fighting and vindictiveness among Catholic factions that emerged in the wake of Vatican II. Liberals and conservatives jump at each other's throats. Bishops disagree. Theologians are silenced. People in parishes argue over whether money should be spent on a new building project when people live in poverty.

Yet these kinds of disagreements are nothing new. Disagreements between German immigrants and Irish immigrants in the Catholic Church during the late 1800's turned into a crisis that threatened to split the American Church when an Irish-American bishop urged immigrants to give up old religious practices and blend into the American melting pot. In the 1930's, 40's and 50's, Catholic factions fought over racial justice issues, with some Catholics actually defending institutional policies that barred Blacks from Catholic hospitals, schools, parishes, convents and even the priesthood.

The ethnic and racial in-fighting was settled over time, just as today's infighting between liberals and conservatives will someday be settled and new issues will rise up with new tensions. The harsh reality is that when people choose to return to the Catholic Church because they feel drawn back by a spiritual pull, they must also accept the human part of the Church with all of the disagreements, the diversity, the darkness and the light. Sometimes it means overlooking the flaws of others. Sometimes it means letting go of pain or anger from the past. Sometimes that's not as easy as it sounds.

Chapter Notes

"We had to show them the Church Christ founded...": Frank Sheed, *The Church and I*, New York: Doubleday & Company, Inc., 1974, pp. 46-63.

"And it is some kind of miracle...": William J. O'Malley, SJ, "The Church of the Faithful," *America*, June 19, 1993, p. 10.

"As I have told hundreds of audiences...": Sheed, p. 339.

"It is well to remind ourselves of St. Paul...": C.G. Jung, *Psychological Reflections*, edited by Jolande Jacobi and R.F.C. Hull, Princeton, New Jersey: Princeton University Press, 1970, p. 253.

Early Christians, for instance...: Peter De Rosa, *Vicars of Christ: The Dark Side of the Papacy*, New York: Crown Publishers, 1988.

"Acknowledging the weakness of the past...": John Paul II, "Tertio Millennio Adveniente," # 33, November, 1994.

In the late 1700's, when the United States was forming...: Harold A. Buetow, *The Catholic School: Its Roots, Identity, and Future*, New York: Crossroad, 1988, p. 22.

CHAPTER 12

Painful Memories

"As a child I was a lector at children's Masses and a folk group member. When my family moved, my mother approached the new pastor and said that I used to do this and would be interested in helping out. The pastor flatly and rudely told her that I would not be wanted in that capacity and no young ladies knew how to behave in that role. It was very hard to be rejected for what God made me — a girl." *Eilish Maura*

"I was abused by a priest as a twelve year old altar boy. The priest who molested me did the same thing to at least 10 other kids that I know in my parish alone, and that's not counting the other places he was assigned." *R.N.*

"I was raped at 15 by someone I knew. I was too frightened to tell either of my parents what had happened. Shortly after the rape, I went to confession for some help. The priest was about 70, and he told me that it was my fault. When I insisted I did not provoke the rape, he refused to give me absolution, and said I was damned to hell and could not be forgiven for what happened. I left the confessional in tears. I know better now, but it still haunts me." *A.G.*

During the 1950's, one nun terrorized an entire generation of second graders in the small town of Williamsville, New York.

The local pediatrician traced all of his seven-year-old bed wetters, thumb suckers, and early morning stomach aches to this nun's class. Years later, a woman admitted that she accidentally discovered the nun's tombstone while cutting through the cemetery. She checked to make sure no one was looking and then spat on the grave.

At any Come Home session you'll hear these same kind of horror stories.

- A man shook with anger as he told about the recurring nightmares his 8-year-old daughter endured after a priest screamed at her in confession.

- A woman's face turned beet red as she relived the humiliation of being publicly denied Communion at her sister's wedding. The priest, who forced everyone in the wedding party to go to confession to him after the rehearsal the night before, refused to give her absolution when she admitted that she and her husband had decided to use birth control until he finished graduate school. The next morning, the priest refused to give her Communion.

During the winter of 1996, the horror stories on America Online's Catholic Message Board were so painful that Father Bob Hughes posted the following message:

> "I have to tell you that as a priest, it is a most difficult thing to hear that the Church or priests or sisters have hurt people in such ways that they no longer can be or feel a part of the Church. I cannot answer for other priests, but I want you to know that there are many of us out there who do indeed care about you."

Some of the most compassionate priests are the ones who overcame painful experiences in their own lives. Msgr. William Stanton has his own horror story about a 6th grade nun, who slapped him across the face when he told her that his grandfather had died the night before. "Were you too proud to ask for prayers for your grandfather when he was sick?" the nun screamed.

"My grandfather wasn't sick," Msgr. Stanton recalls. "But I didn't say anything to her. Later that morning, another nun came to the door and told her that my grandfather dropped dead when he knelt down to say his prayers."

As Msgr. Stanton speaks, you can see traces of a young boy's pain in his eyes, and yet, he never internalized the incident in a way that made him turn away from God or the Church. "Maybe it was because my father was so strong in the faith," he suggests. "Or maybe it is because I have very good memories of other nuns."

Father John Catoir admits that while going to confession as a young teenager a priest sexually abused him. "He touched me inappropriately. It was such a shock that I recoiled in horror, but I told no one. I went home and cried for an hour. I went back later and confronted him, but he brushed it off. I forgave him a long time ago, but I never forgot."

Father Paul Nogaro recalls the pain of being the only Italian in a Catholic grammar school that was largely German. "There was a theft and the pastor focused on me because I was Italian. I was totally innocent, but if you were not German in this parish you were suspect. It was very hurtful and I suppose I could have turned against the Church, but I didn't for some reason. Maybe it has to do with personality and psychology. Some people are very fragile. Other people will say, 'I don't care what you do to me. Nothing is going to turn me away from the Church.'"

Father Andrew Greeley might fit into the second category. His own struggle with the institutional Church has not been easy, and yet he refuses to abandon what he calls the Catholic Christian heritage. The central question, he insists, is whether or not Catholicism is true. If you believe Catholicism is true, it doesn't matter one iota how anyone else, including nuns and priests, live out the truth of Catholicism. It only matters how you live out that truth.

Many times, the simple act of unburdening hurts at a Come Home program enables people to take another look at their relationship with God and the Church. Other times, it requires a specific action, like spitting on a nun's grave, to release the pent up pain. Some people simply come to the realization that it's time to accept what happened in the past and move on.

> "A priest told my mother that she had to stop using birth control, and she died the following year during childbirth. I've been mad at that priest for almost 30 years. I can see now that my anger affected my whole life and all the decisions I made. It's time to let that anger go." *K.D.*

One of the most healing factors for many people is the discovery that there are nuns and priests in the Church who actually care about their pain and want to help them come back.

> "I hated nuns, but it was a nun that led me back to the Church. She was in charge of grieving families in the parish where my mother was buried. She didn't fit the image of the nuns that I had in grammar school. When she called a few weeks after the funeral to ask how we were doing, I had a long talk with her. She was instrumental in my decision to return to the Church." *M.H.*

Father Flavian Walsh, OFM, finds himself continually apologizing in the name of the "Church" for stupidity, vindictiveness, cruelty, abuse, and pain. He never questions the truthfulness of a person's story or the amount of pain that the incident caused. He never says, "Oh, that couldn't possibly have happened." He sometimes suggests that a person try to redirect the anger at the Church-person, who hurt them, and not at the whole Church.

He recalls a woman whose brother committed suicide. At

the cemetery, the priest told her, "This was a waste of good prayers. Your brother is in hell."

"That priest was wrong," Father Flavian says. "He had no right to make that kind of judgment."

Hearing a priest admit that another priest was wrong can be an incredibly healing experience. The woman who was refused Communion at her sister's wedding stood speechless when she learned that a priest cannot publicly refuse Communion to anyone, and in her case the priest may have violated canon law by using information he had heard in confession against her.

It took several priests and a number of lay people to reassure the woman who was told in confession that she was damned to hell because she had been raped. She later learned that the priest had suffered a stroke around that time. "That's probably part of the reason I got the advice that I did," she admits.

Sometimes, people's struggles with the Church intertwine themselves with painful situations in their own families that might include anger, arguing, violence, abuse, or alcoholism.

> "My father was an alcoholic. He would get drunk and abusive every night, but on Sunday morning he would be in Church acting as if he were the holiest man in the world. It was disgusting." *C.M., New York*

Father Andrew Greeley suggests that sometimes people break away from Catholicism as an unconscious protest against their parents. They turn God into a surrogate father and the Church into a surrogate mother, and blame religion for bad things that happened in their families. When they dig deeper, they realize that their reasons for leaving the Church are more a function of their problems with their parents than problems with the Church.

Father William F. McKee, CSSR, who has worked with almost 10,000 inactive Catholics over the past fourteen years, agrees: "Many of the inactive Catholics for whom I worked were aching. In most, the cause of their disenchantment with the Church was, not the Church, but that life had let them down, shattered their hope. As a result, they hurt. Personal failure, mishaps, loss, death, and/or destruction of dreams might have singly or collectively contributed to their pain. They had to blame someone; and often enough they blamed the Church — the priests, the bishops, the pope — anyone who had represented God during their growing-up years."

For others, the pain is much more complicated. Certainly, some of the darkest shadows in today's Church are incidents of sexual abuse of children by clergy.

> "I would like to know why priests can commit terrible sins and still say Mass. I find it very hard to involve myself in the Church knowing priests are living 'lies.' How can a priest teach the words of God and not live by them?" *B.F.*

The reality is most priests do try to live the Gospel message. A recent commission in the Archdiocese of Chicago reviewed clergy files for sexual allegations made in the last 25 years, and found valid accusations against only 39 priests, which accounted for 5% of the priests in the diocese. Some were dead or had left the priesthood. The remaining 21 were removed from active service.

While cases of abuse are found in the ranks of Protestant and Jewish clergy, public school teachers, coaches, youth counselors and other professions, allegations against priests receive the most media attention because, as Cardinal Joseph Bernardin remarked, their celibate commitment calls them to a higher standard. Cardinal Bernardin also proved that some accusations of sexual abuse are false. In 1993, Steven Cook, a former seminarian, accused Bernardin of sexual misconduct. Cook later rescinded the claim, and the Cardinal's openness in forgiving him led Cook to a reconciliation with the Church before he died from AIDS in 1995.

A recent survey in the *Boston Globe* shows that while Catholics express anger over abuse cases, they also report no loss of faith in their Catholic beliefs. "I won't let them take my faith away from me," the mother of one victim insisted.

Some people express outrage at bishops for inept handling of these problems, but others acknowledge that until the mid-1980's even mental health professionals knew very little about sexual abuse, and because abuse is always clouded in secrecy, no one knew the extent of the problem.

"I can honestly say that I never knew this was happening," says Father James Hennesey, SJ, who served in administrative positions for the Jesuits throughout the past 40 years. "I am not saying that it didn't happen, but I never saw it, and I was shocked when all of this began to surface."

After meeting with a dozen victims of abuse during the November 1992 meeting of the U.S. Bishops in Washington, Los Angeles Cardinal Roger Mahoney told the 275 bishops that listening to the survivors was "one of the most moving experiences" he had ever known. "The Church [must] show herself as a loving, caring and healing Church and not as a legal obstacle protecting errant priests."

Today, many dioceses approach the problem directly. Father Robert Zapfel helped design one of the first "pro-active" programs to fight abuse by educating people in the Church who work with children to recognize signs of abuse and to report it. He was also part of a team of psychologists, social workers, and health care professionals who go into parishes where abuse has been uncovered. "Our first concern is making sure that those who were in danger are no longer at risk," he says.

The second thing is to begin the healing process as quickly as possible. If a child is abused it is not just the child's issue. It is a family issue. Parents and siblings are offered help. Everyone needs to deal with this tragic situation.

The third thing is getting help for the abuser. A lot of people want us to punish that individual. We always remove the person from the parish, and we cooperate with civil authorities. But the Church also recognizes that this is a person with a mental, emotional and spiritual illness which has to be addressed in a professional way. We need to stop this cycle of abuse.

Finally, we have to speak openly about the problem of abuse from the pulpit. It's difficult because in a congregation you have kids, senior citizens, people who are aware of the problem, and people who don't know what you're talking about. But it can be done. Whenever I have addressed this issue from the pulpit, I have had a long line waiting after Mass to thank me. People need to hear it. Not every priest is able to do it, but we need to enable more priests to speak openly about these problems.

In the past ten years, several support groups for victims of abuse have sprung up around the country. Frank Fitzpatrick, who was abused by James Porter, started Survivor Connections. Jeanne Miller founded Victims of Clergy Abuse Linkup after a priest tried to abuse her son. Barbara Blaine, who was molested by a parish priest from age 13 to age 17, formed SNAP (Survivors Network for those Abused by Priests).

Barbara Blaine never stopped being Catholic. "My faith is in my blood," she says. "It gives me life. It nourishes me. It's my hope for the future."

Unlike Barbara, many victims of clergy abuse struggle with their faith because their most painful memories are tied to things that were done to them by someone who represented God or threatened them with God's punishment.

Madeleine L'Engle once wrote: "We don't 'get over' the deepest pains of life, nor should we... we learn to live with them, to go on growing and deepening our understanding that God can come into all our pain, and make something creative out of it."

Can God make something creative out of something as devastating as sexual abuse? Yes, says a woman who suffered abuse by a priest. "The first step is moving from victim to survivor. Now I am beyond the survivor stage and consider myself an advocate for others who were abused and are still silent."

It may seem hard to believe that the movement from victim to survivor to advocate is possible. For many people, the transition will require the help of a professional counselor or a recovery support group. Some people suggest that the process of spiritual healing can help.

> "I know I have to forgive if I want to feel whole and peaceful again. But how do you forgive when it hurts so much?" *S.J.*

Chapter Notes

Father Andrew Greeley might fit into the second category…: John J. Delaney, Editor, *Why Catholic?*, New York: Doubleday & Company, Inc. 1979, p. 60-61.

A recent commission in the Archdiocese of Chicago…: Andrew M. Greeley, "How Serious is the Problem of Sexual Abuse by Clergy?", *America*, March 20, 1993, pp. 6-10.

A recent survey in the *Boston Globe*…: *Ibid.*

"I won't let them take my faith away…": *Ibid.*

"one of the most moving experiences…": and ff. Jason Berry, "Listening to the Survivors: Voices of People of God," *America*, November 13, 1993.

"My faith is in my blood…": Tim Unsworth, *Catholics on the Edge*, New York: Crossroad, 1995, p. 71.

"The first step is moving from victim to survivor…": Jason Berry, *op. cit.*

CHAPTER 13

How to Forgive when It Hurts So Much

"How do you forgive someone who lied to you, manipulated you, used you, abused you, and then abandoned you?" *S.W.*

"I am struggling with some very un-Christian feelings toward my husband's ex-wife. I'm not sure how I can ever forgive her." *B.E., Virginia*

"Every time I think I've truly forgiven, painful memories from the past resurface and it's like the whole thing is happening all over again. Is there any way to break out of this cycle?" *P.B.*

Father John Catoir tells the story of a priest, who was walking from the garage to the rectory one evening when a drug addict with a knife came up behind him and said, "Give me your wallet."

The priest responded by inviting the man in to have some coffee and talk, but the drug addict was desperate. They scuffled, and the priest was stabbed repeatedly. Finally, the man got the wallet and ran. The priest ended up with stitches in his face, arm and side. When Father Catoir had dinner with him a few weeks later, he asked, "Have you been able to forgive that guy?"

"I must have forgiven him a million times," the priest replied, "but I still wake up in the middle of the night wrestling with him!"

"The point of the story is that the priest did forgive the man who attacked him," Father Catoir says. "He knew that he had forgiven because forgiveness is in the will, but his feelings hadn't caught up yet. About a year later I asked him about it and he said the feelings had started to subside."

When Father Catoir says forgiveness is in the will, he means that when we forgive we make a clear, free decision to forgive, whether we feel like forgiving or not. You may intensely dislike this person. You may not ever want to see this person again. The person may not want your forgiveness. The person may not deserve your forgiveness. But you choose to forgive anyway.

Why? Because by choosing to forgive, you set free your anger, resentment, frustration and thoughts of revenge. Forgiveness is good for you. It allows you to let the poison drain out of the wound so that it can begin to heal.

"If we are a prisoner of our past hurts — no matter how profound and how deep — we are a prisoner nonetheless," says Father Robert Zapfel. "The Lord came to set prisoners free. He meant people unjustly behind bars, but sometimes those bars are bars of jealousy, resentment, hatred, lack of forgiveness, lack of compassion, lack of charity in our lives. The freedom to be open to God's love means being free from those kinds of prison bars as well."

In the Gospels Jesus tells us to forgive our enemies. When Peter asks if it is enough to forgive seven times, Jesus tells him to forgive seventy times seven. Jesus also assured us that if we forgive, we will be forgiven for our failings. In the Lord's Prayer, Jesus taught us to ask God to forgive our trespasses "as we forgive those who trespass against us." On the cross, Jesus showed us how to forgive when he prayed, "Father, forgive them for they know not what they do."

It's not easy to forgive. It is not something that happens instantaneously. It is a process that begins with your desire to forgive, but sometimes you have to keep reminding yourself that this is something you really want to do. Sometimes you have to say out loud: *I want to forgive. I want to let go of this pain.*

Praying for the person you're trying to forgive can help — especially if it is a person you have frequent contact with and you find yourself constantly filled with anger or resentment. "Say a Hail Mary each time you see that person or think about that person," Father Catoir suggests. "That will be your sign to God that you want to forgive, and you'll be at peace knowing that you are trying."

It doesn't hurt to pray for yourself, too. Ask God to help you forgive — especially when painful memories surface. Say, "Lord, heal me. Don't let me wallow in this." Sometimes people write out their anger and frustration in a letter to the person, and then burn what they wrote. As the smoke rises, they see it as a symbol of the negative feelings that they are giving to God.

Confession can also be part of the healing if someone goes to a priest and says, "I've been so angry and so hurt for so long that I have to confess this."

Father John Powell, SJ, says going over his own faults helps him to forgive others. "Some of the things I have done and some things I should have done but failed to do remain clouded in mystery for me. 'Why did I ever do that? Why did I ever say that? Why didn't I keep my promise? How could I have been so blind?' I am reminded that in our own self-knowledge we know only the tip of the iceberg. Under the waves of our lives are many unseen influences that so easily throw us off balance. Now if this is true of you and me, it's true of all others who need our forgiveness; they may not know why they did or said whatever it was."

James and Evelyn Whitehead, who facilitate workshops on how to deal with negative emotions, point out that forgiveness will not wipe the slate clean and allow us to act as if nothing happened. "Something *has* happened, something profound. The fabric of our interwoven lives has been torn. Yet we can choose not to be defined by this rupture, incorporating it instead as a part of an ongoing relationship."

The late Father Lawrence Martin Jenco, OSM, who was held hostage in Lebanon for 564 days, forgave the terrorists from the very first day, but he never forgot what happened: "People say, 'Oh, forgive and forget' as if it's a mandate from God. But it doesn't work that way. I have all kinds of memories, and when I recall, I heal. It's important to realize that you just can't forgive and forget — it's contrary to human nature. Allow the memories to come forth, to look at them, and heal. Say, 'God, heal that for me or allow me not to get caught up in it.' You must ask God for that gift. We are constantly going to God to ask for forgiveness, so why don't we ask God for the generosity to forgive as God forgives."

In trying to forgive, some people discover that they really don't want to let go of the pain, the anger or the resentment. On some subconscious level, they relish the role of the injured party.

> "I remember praying one night that the Lord would take away all the painful memories from the past. I can't explain it, but suddenly, it seemed like chunks of my past started falling away. At first I felt so free, but then I realized that I didn't want to release the resentment I had toward certain people and I didn't want certain wounds healed. I was using those things as excuses for my moods, my personality and why I did some of the things that I did. If those things were taken away, what could I blame?" *H.L., New York*

"We have all met people who have 'been dead' their whole lives because they have never been able, or willing, to break free from hurts inflicted or endured," writes Father Paul Wadell, CP, an ethics professor at Catholic Theological Union in Chicago.

"Their guilt grows, their sorrow absorbs them, their anger, however just, begins to define them. All of us, when we are wronged or when we do wrong, can go away and bury ourselves in guilt, denial, sadness, anger, or resentment, leaving our hearts so dead that it seems they can never be resurrected. Or, we can begin the challenging, sometimes painful, but always promising journey to reconciliation and new life."

> "I came from a family that was very unforgiving. There was a lot of anger in our house and blaming. The same with the nuns at school. I was always afraid of getting yelled at in church, in school, and at home. Whenever something bad happens, it's like a little voice in my head that keeps saying, 'This is all your fault.'"
> G.K., *Massachusetts*

Sometimes in working through our anger and resentment, we discover layers of attitudes or influences from the past that subconsciously affect our feelings and behavior today. If you're trying to let go of something that happened in the past, ask yourself what inner messages influence you.

In his theory of transactional analysis, Eric Berne suggests that there are three elements struggling inside of us: the *parent*, which is a replay of the rules we learned from authority figures; the *child*, which includes all of our feelings and emotional responses; the *adult*, which involves our ability as a mature person to use our intellect and our will in formulating how we will act and react.

"We must never let the messages on our parent tapes or the emotions of the child in us make decisions for us," says Father John Powell, SJ. "I must always keep the adult in me in charge — my mind thinking independently and my will choosing the course of behavior for itself. I must decide how I am going to act. And I must take full responsibility for my actions."

Let's suppose, for example, that the parent (or nun or priest) inside you is negative, accusing, threatening, punishing or abusive. The child in you will react with defensiveness, guilt, fear, defiance, or pain. In order to stop this negative internal process, the adult in you has to step in and say, "I am not a bad person. God loves me. I don't care what anyone says or does. Nothing is going to turn me away from the Church if I decide to come back."

When dealing with deep-seated pain from the past, some priests suggest spiritual healing, which is essentially the process of asking Jesus Christ to walk with us back to the time when we were hurt, and free us from the pain. Msgr. Vincent Becker has used this process successfully with people who want to let go of painful memories:

> Basically, what I do is put my hands on a person's head, and ask the Lord to remove the pain of the past and replace it with his love. I have worked with people who have been abused. I tell them, "You just can't forget something so awful. You can't deny this happened. You have to admit that this really happened, and this was awful, and it was the most traumatic thing in your whole life. What this other person did was sinful and wrong. God knows you've suffered. God suffered through this horrible traumatic thing with you. God didn't abandon you."
>
> If a person can get to the point of saying, "I want to do whatever Jesus wants me to do," then the person can begin the process of forgiving. This is an immense step from unfreedom to freedom, and if you can make that step, your whole life is no longer tied and bound to the fact that 25 years ago you were a victim.
>
> You can't take it all away, and it's not like all of a sudden you will forget. You allow the abuse to take its place in your life, but not to dominate your life.

This kind of healing is pure grace that comes to us from God. We begin the process by expressing our desire to forgive, but the healing is a gift. "There is something divine about forgiveness," writes Catherine de Hueck Doherty. "It is truly and closely aligned to charity, to love, to God himself."

When St. Therese of Lisieux found herself constantly irritated by one of the other nuns to the point where she felt as if she simply could not tolerate this woman any longer, she turned to God. She knew that God wanted her to love this woman, but she simply could not love this nun on a human level, so she asked God to love the other nun through her. Essentially, she told God that because she could not conjure the feelings of love, she would serve as the instrument through which God could love the other nun.

Eileen Dunn of Boothwyn, Pennsylvania did the same thing when she found herself engulfed in feelings of hatred toward a man she knew. "I finally gave up trying to love that man on my own," she explains. "Instead, I set aside extra prayer time just for that situation. I simply sat before the Lord and asked Him to remove the hatred by filling me completely with himself. Over the next few days, I could actually feel my mood changing. It felt as though someone had turned the heat down under a pot that was boiling over. I found that I was able to talk to that man without cringing… I kept praying, and almost imperceptibly my feelings went through stages from hatred to calm acceptance to love."

> "I told God that I wanted to forgive everyone in my life who had hurt me. It didn't happen all at once. I kept praying and asking God to take away the anger and resentment. Gradually, I realized that God was filling me with a deep inner peace that I can't describe other than to say it heals me, and sustains me, and helps me see things from a different perspective." D.L., *New York*

Chapter Notes

"Some of the things I have done...": John Powell, SJ, *Through the Eyes of Faith*, Allen, Texas: Tabor Publishing, 1992, pp. 138-143.

"Something has happened, something profound...": James D. Whitehead and Evelyn Eaton Whitehead, *Shadows of the Heart*, New York: Crossroad Publishing Co., 1994, p. 85.

"People say, 'Oh, forgive and forget...'": "Forgive and Don't Forget," The Editors interview Father Lawrence Martin Jenco, OSM, *U.S. Catholic*, March 1996, pp. 8-10.

"We have all met people who have 'been dead'...": Father Paul Wadell, CP, "Forgiveness is a Hard Act to Follow," *U.S. Catholic*, August, 1996, p. 36.

"We must never let the messages...": John Powell, SJ, *Solving the Riddle of Self*, Allen, Texas: Tabor Publishing, 1995, p. 61.

"There is something divine about forgiveness...": Catherine de Hueck Doherty, *Dearly Beloved: Letters to the Children of My Spirit*, Vol. 3, Combermere, Ontario: Madonna House Publications, 1990, p. 132

"I finally gave up trying...": Eileen Dunn, "The Toughest Test: Loving Those Hard to Love," *New Covenant*, October 1995, p. 17.

CHAPTER 14

A Look Inside the Marriage Tribunal

"I am divorced from my husband who was an alcoholic among other things. I've been to confession and consider myself forgiven. Because I made a mistake when I was young, will I be penalized all my life? It is my understanding that an annulment is a very difficult and costly process and I feel that my ex-husband would be a problem just to spite me. He is very manipulative and would lie just to cause me pain." *A.D.*

"I am intimidated by the annulment process. My ex-husband says he will support my annulment because the marriage never meant anything to him anyway and he admits that he never wanted children. But I'm embarrassed to ask friends to write on my behalf. Why does the tribunal need witnesses?" *R.C., Connecticut*

"Would feeling coerced to marry qualify for an annulment? Would the fact that my spouse's parents dictated most of the marriage be grounds? What about an abusive spouse? I've endured all three of these situations in my brief four year marriage." *L.S., California*

In his best selling novel, *Beach Music*, Pat Conroy creates a scene where a mother tells her adult son that the Catholic Church has annulled her marriage to his alcoholic father.

Shocked and outraged, the son wants to know how the Church can say the marriage never happened. What about all the pain of his childhood? Does that no longer exist, too? Are he and his brothers now considered bastards?

> "Why did you raise me in such a ridiculous, brain-dead, dimwitted, sexually perverse, odd-duck, know-nothing, silly-assed Church?"
> "I raised my children in the Cadillac of religions," said Lucy.
> "We're not your real children... The marriage was annulled. You can forget about morning sickness, the pain of childbirth, messy placentas, two o'clock feedings, measles, chicken pox... none of it happened. Your kids are five little nightmares you never had."
> "The Cadillac," she said. "The top of the line."

Annulments tend to evoke strong feelings, and like the angry son in *Beach Music*, much of the pain and negativity stems from misconceptions. An ecclesiastical annulment is not a Catholic divorce. It does not mean a loving marital relationship never existed. It does not make the children illegitimate. It does not have to be processed in Rome, and you don't have to have power or influence to obtain one. Most cases take 6 to 10 months, although some may take up to two years because of complexities or heavy case loads at the local tribunal. The length of the marriage or the number of children are not factors in the decision. Tribunals do not worry about the number of annulments granted each month. There is no quota system. Each case is handled on an individual basis. It does not cost thousands of dollars; in fact the average fee is $300-$600, which covers less than half of the actual administrative costs. No case is ever refused because of financial difficulties.

The reason so much emphasis is placed on the annulment process is that the Catholic Church takes very seriously the words of Jesus in the Gospels that prohibit divorce and remarriage (Mt 5:31-32, Mk 10:11-12, Lk 16:18). The Church teaches that a valid sacramental marriage is indissoluble except by the death of one spouse. An annulment is an official declaration by a Church tribunal that when the marriage took place there was no valid sacramental marriage bond because of an impediment or lack of consent on the part of one or both parties.

"An annulment means that from day one, no matter how good that marriage looked on the surface, way back at the very beginning when the couple exchanged vows, there were impediments so big that at least one of them could not make a mature, adult commitment to the marriage," explains Msgr. Vincent Becker, a tribunal judge.

For marital consent to be valid, canon law requires that both parties possess sufficient use of reason and a mature understanding of the matrimonial rights and duties. They must have the ability to assume the obligations of marriage without psychological impediments. They must give free consent without pressure or force. They must be willing to bear children, and there must be no deceit or fraud on the part of either party. If any of these impediments are present before or at the time of marriage, grounds for an annulment exist.

For example, if a marriage lasts less than a year, it probably involved a serious lack of maturity. A marriage involving an out-of-wedlock pregnancy raises the question as to whether both parties gave free consent without pressure or force. When there is any history of serious psychological disorders or addictions, there is the possibility that the person was unable to assume the obligations of marriage. If there was an emotional compulsion to marry, such as the desire to get out of the house or fear of family disfavor for not marrying, the validity of consent can be questioned. Maybe there was no real commitment to remain in the marriage for life. Maybe suppressed gay or lesbian tendencies surfaced. Maybe one or both partners lacked the ability to make sound judgments. If there was physical or emotional abuse, questions could be raised as to whether there was a true understanding of the marriage covenant.

The Church also stipulates that for a marriage to be valid, the ceremony must comply with canon law. Catholics who married in a civil ceremony or in a non-Catholic service without a dispensation are often surprised to learn that they don't need an annulment because the Church never did recognize their marriage as valid.

> "I was married by a justice of the peace. My parish priest said my case was considered defect of form. All I needed was my baptismal certificate, my marriage certificate, my divorce decree and $50. Within two weeks, I had the papers saying the marriage was null and void."
> *M.J.F., New York*

Before you can begin the annulment process, you must go through a civil divorce. The next step is to talk to your parish priest or call your diocesan marriage tribunal. You will be asked to complete a questionnaire that details the history of your family, your courtship, your marriage and the reasons for your divorce. It is very important to be honest about yourself and your ex-spouse. Be sure to mention any nervous disorders, psychiatric care, addictions, promiscuity, abuse, fraud, or factors that may have pressured one or both parties into marrying. The purpose of this information is not to place blame on either party, but to seek the truth.

> "I tried twice to go through the annulment process. Both times I got hung up on having to write a detailed description of my relationship with my parents and my sex life before and during the marriage." *Rebecca Oliver, California*

Others insist, however, that the process is therapeutic because it helped them let go of old baggage and get on with their lives.

> "To say the annulment process is painful is certainly an understatement, but I think the Church is providing

healing for those of us who have gone through a divorce. As painful as it was, the annulment process helped me come to peace with the past." *Angela Southerland, Fayetteville, North Carolina*

Sometimes local parishes or diocesan offices have the names of priests or lay people who are familiar with the annulment process and can help you with your paperwork. "When people come to me, I tell them to keep in mind that the Church is looking for attitude and maturity at the time of marriage," says Msgr. Becker.

If a woman puts down that her husband was a heavy drinker in their marriage, I might ask her to think of some examples in courtship when he got drunk. I look to see if the pattern was set way back there and maybe she didn't see it. Most of the time she saw it, but she didn't put any tag on it. The drinking seemed like fun. She'll say they were party people when they were young, but he never changed. He never grew up the way she expected that he would. In reality, he was probably already addicted.

We see that with drugs, too. Sometimes the petitioner knew or suspected that the fiancée was using drugs and was slightly bothered by it, but when it came to a point in the marriage when the person's behavior and way of functioning changed, it caused problems.

It's the same with sexual infidelity. A woman getting married might know that her partner cheated on her once in a while during their courtship, but then it gets worse.

Often the grounds are defective consent due to a lack of mature judgment on the part of *both* parties. That might seem strange to the average person, but what it really comes down to is this: *If the other person in the marriage was as bad as you say, why didn't you see it back then?* The defective consent or immature judgment on your part hinges on: *I should have known better.*

If you find that writing the history is too difficult, try talking your answers into a tape recorder or letting a friend interview you. Then transcribe the tape. The important thing is to get as much information as possible down on paper. Before you submit your petition to the tribunal, let your parish priest or someone who understands the annulment process look it over.

"When some people write their marital histories, they say to themselves: 'I don't want to write anything bad about my ex-spouse or about myself,'" explains Msgr. William Gallagher, a tribunal judge.

> If I read their paperwork and find nothing substantial in their case history, I'll call them in and ask: "Are you saying your marriage failed for no good reason?"
> "No," they always reply. "There were lots of reasons."
> When I ask what really happened, they will admit that they wanted to get out of the house. They wanted to get away from an abusive father or a dysfunctional family. All their friends were getting married. They thought they could change the other person after they were married. They thought the other person would stop drinking, or stop using drugs, or agree to have children or get a steady job. These are all possible grounds for an annulment, but people have to write that in their petition. The marriage tribunal takes each individual case, compares it to Church law, and makes a judgment based on the facts. Before the process can begin, people have to provide the tribunal with as much background information as possible.

The next crucial step is acceptance or rejection of the case for formal process by the tribunal, which means that if the tribunal thinks that sufficient grounds exist, the case is assigned to a tribunal judge. If not, the tribunal tells you that your petition is denied and you can resubmit your case if additional information becomes available. Many people give up at this point.

"I tried to get an annulment after my husband of 18 years left me to raise our three kids by myself. I tried to tell the tribunal that if my husband would leave me like that then there was probably no love to begin with and an annulment should be granted. They said that is not necessarily so. They wanted me to 'prove' that he didn't love me. How can I prove that? He left, didn't he? What does that tell you?" *W.B., Illinois*

The Church considers a marriage to be valid unless it can be proven otherwise. A tribunal judge may want to believe your story, but in order to justify the case, he needs proof. The fact that some people lie makes the need for proof even more critical.

"For example, suppose a woman abhors the thought of sexual contact, and this only comes to light after the marriage," explains Father John Catoir, a canon lawyer and tribunal judge, who has written books on the annulment process.

Could this be considered fraud that goes to the heart of the marriage contract? More than likely there are psychological problems involved, but proving them is quite another matter. Suppose the couple breaks up, and she refuses to cooperate in an annulment process. How can a tribunal know if the husband is telling the truth? Proof that his wife always felt repulsed at the idea of sexual intercourse is not easy to produce.

Today, the courts use character testimony to establish the credibility of the petitioner. The story the husband tells about his wife is probably true if his credibility is solid. If the husband is a person known to be truthful and of good character, witnesses to that effect can help him.

Once your case is accepted by the tribunal, you will have to arrange for the testimony of witnesses, who can attest to the facts surrounding the marriage and to your truthfulness. It's a good idea to urge your witnesses to tell the truth, no matter how negatively you or your ex-spouse might appear in their story.

You will also have to supply the tribunal with the current address of your ex-spouse, who will be contacted by the tribunal.

> "I was married to a man who was so abusive that he almost killed me. I had to get a court order to keep him away because he was stalking me. I know I have grounds for an annulment, but the diocese insists that I give them the name and address of my ex-husband. If they contact him, he will start thinking about me again." *D.B.*

The Church insists that a former spouse has the right to offer his or her own testimony, but there is no need for the two of you to have any personal contact. In cases where an ex-spouse is abusive or threatening, a judge will make a notation on the file and questions directed at your spouse will be stated as generally as possible with no direct reference to your testimony.

> "I was told that my former spouse had three choices: He could cooperate in the proceedings and present his side of the story to the tribunal. He could ignore the proceedings, which after some time, would cause the tribunal to decide the case based upon my testimony and that of my witnesses. Or, he could fight the procedure. At first, he decided to ignore it. However, the day before his deadline to respond, he decided to fight it, even though he had remarried outside the Church. The Judge in my case called him up and eventually talked him into cooperating. The Church granted me the declaration of nullity on the basis of defect of consent." *Debbie Paul, California*

During the process, you will have the opportunity to meet privately with the judge assigned to your case. Some tribunals will also appoint an advocate to help you with your case.

> "I work with a Diocesan Marriage Tribunal and I'm sure

that ours is similar to those in most dioceses in the United States," says Father Bob Hughes. "They are filled with men and women, priests and lay people who are compassionate and non-judgmental. We seek to bring justice and peace into the lives of people who are hurting."

While tribunals in different dioceses will have different case loads, and slightly different ways of managing their offices, all tribunals must comply with the official procedures set down by canon law. Remember, however, that tribunals are staffed by human beings, who sometimes get bogged down or make mistakes.

> "In my diocese, there was a backlog of over 400 cases, and then the judge lost our papers. I would offer the following recommendations to anyone starting the annulment process:
>
> • retain a copy of any paperwork provided to the tribunal.
>
> • Even though witnesses usually do not share their paperwork with you, ask them to retain a copy in case the original gets lost.
>
> • Keep a log of when you receive paperwork from the tribunal and log when you forward paperwork or documents to them. If you need to write for other documents (divorce decrees, Church records, etc.) keep a copy of the dated requests.
>
> • Read up on the procedure. Ask questions.
>
> • Call once a month and ask to speak to the judge handling your case. This is to see where you are, but more important, if the diocese has an overload of cases, this forces the judge to retrieve your folder from a drawer, review it, and if possible take the next step. In my diocese, the cases completed first are brought to a decision. Theoretically, you could file first, but if someone else gets their paperwork in and all their supporting

documentation, their case will be handled before yours. This is why you want someone to keep looking at your case once a month — to see what is missing and let everyone know you're serious and looking for a decision." *K.M.D., New Jersey*

If your case receives an affirmative decision from the tribunal, it will automatically be sent to a second tribunal for review. If both tribunals agree, you will receive a decree of nullity. If your case receives a negative decision from the tribunal, you may appeal the decision. If the second court also votes "negative" then that case may never be opened on the same grounds. You may, however, submit a new case on different grounds or appeal to Rome.

It would be nice to say that the annulment process solves everyone's problems, but life doesn't work that way. In the next chapter, we'll look at some of the options available for people who can't get an annulment for one reason or another.

Chapter Notes

"Why did you raise me in such a ridiculous...": Pat Conroy, *Beach Music*, New York: Doubleday, 1995, pp. 337-338.

When there is any history of serious psychological disorders...: Regarding psychological grounds (canon 1095) it is not enough that a psychological problem would make marriage difficult, rather it must be grave enough to make it nearly impossible. It must be something that is present at the time of consent, at least in an incipient stage. Neuroses are present everywhere and are usually not sufficient to indicate incapacity. In most cases, evidence from psychological experts is necessary.

If any of these impediments are present...: Code of Canon Law, canons 1095-1107.

"For example, suppose a woman...": John T. Catoir, *Where Do You Stand with the Church?*, Staten Island: Alba House, 1996.

CHAPTER 15

The Dilemma of Divorced and Remarried Catholics

"My annulment was denied because my ex-husband refused to cooperate. I did nothing wrong. My husband left me. Last year, I married a man who loves me and accepts my kids. The Church instantly turned its back on me. I was told not to come to Communion. My name was removed from the lector's list. Why does the Church treat people like this? What purpose does it serve to deny me my Catholic birthright? What happened to Jesus' message of forgiveness, mercy and compassion?" *W.B., Illinois*

"I have been married now for 15 years to a Protestant, who was divorced before I met him. Lately, I have been attending Mass and a weekly novena. The Catholic Church is the only one for me, but I feel unwelcome because it has been so long and my marriage is not recognized. Many years ago, a priest told me to follow my heart and conscience about receiving Communion. Please give me some advice." *B.J., Florida*

"I married my husband in a civil ceremony with the understanding that he was a practicing Catholic and would get an annulment from his alcoholic wife, but now he says we can receive the sacraments without the annulment." *S.M.L.*

127

"I read a book that presented a view that some divorced Catholics take Communion anyway and that we are allowed to use our own discernment. That's almost heresy, isn't it?" *C.R.J.*

At almost every Come Home session, someone will stand up and say, "If I murdered my 'ex,' I could go to Confession and receive Communion, but I did the humane thing; I got divorced, and then I married the person I should have married in the first place. The Church can forgive everything else, but they can't forgive people who are divorced and remarried."

Sometimes the person making this statement is angry and frustrated. Sometimes the person is on the verge of tears. But the underlying feelings of alienation, rejection and hopelessness are the same.

Is there a place for divorced and remarried Catholics in the Catholic Church?

In 1981, Pope John Paul II issued a strongly worded statement saying "yes," there is a place:

> The Church, which was set up to lead to salvation all people and especially the baptized, cannot abandon to their own devices those who have been previously bound by sacramental marriage and who have attempted a second marriage. The Church will therefore make untiring efforts to put at their disposal her means of salvation.
>
> Pastors must know that for the sake of truth they are obliged to exercise careful discernment of situations. There is, in fact, a difference between those who have sincerely tried to save their first marriage and have been unjustly abandoned and those who, through their own grave fault, have destroyed a canonically valid marriage.
>
> Finally, there are those who have entered into a second union for the sake of the children's upbringing and who are sometimes subjectively certain in conscience that

their previous irreparably destroyed marriage had never been valid.

Together with the synod, I earnestly call upon pastors and the whole community of the faithful to help the divorced and with solicitous care to make sure that they do not consider themselves as separated from the Church, for as baptized persons they can and indeed must share in her life. They should be encouraged to listen to the word of God, to attend the sacrifice of the Mass, to persevere in prayer, to contribute to works of charity and to the community effort in favor of justice, to bring up their children in the Christian faith, to cultivate the spirit and practice of penance and thus implore, day by day, God's grace. Let the Church pray for them, encourage them and show herself a merciful mother and thus sustain them in faith and hope.

The Pope goes on, however, to reaffirm the Church's teaching on the indissolubility of marriage and states unequivocally that people living in invalid marriages "cannot be admitted to the Eucharist." In September, 1994, the Congregation for the Doctrine of the Faith issued a letter to the bishops reaffirming this position.

"After I remarried, I played the organ at Masses for six years without receiving Communion, and I can tell you that it hurts. There is nothing quite as devastating as exclusion from the Eucharist." *B.W.*

"People say it's like having spiritual leprosy," says Msgr. Vincent Becker. "In my old parish, we had two center pews, but on the far sides there were smaller pews which only three people could get into. Some people told me they would sit over on the sides so it wouldn't look that bad if they didn't go to Communion. The first time I heard this I realized how hard this was for people."

Some find it easier to stand in the back of the church or to leave Mass early. They find it upsetting when ushers try to force them to move to a front pew. It's even worse when a priest reprimands those who leave early for not staying until the last note of the last song. Many people simply stop going to Mass.

> "I can't stand to sit through Mass and not receive Communion. It's not that I feel conspicuous as there are plenty of others who stay behind, it's just that it hurts to be separated." C.R.J.

If you are living in an invalid second marriage, you already know the feelings of rejection and probably have painful stories of your own. What you might not know is that several options remain open to you, some of which might work, and some which won't.

As a first step, most priests would encourage you to take another look at the possibility of an annulment — even if the tribunal previously rejected your case or denied your annulment.

> "As a divorced, lapsed Catholic for 24 years, I figured it would be impossible, but with the help of a wonderful priest, I was able to wind my way through the annulment maze and am now back." Gene Kinnaly, Jacksonville, Florida

In the past 10 to 15 years, marriage tribunals have radically altered their procedures and expanded the grounds for annulments to include psychological factors that were previously unknown. Today, there is even a possibility in cases where an ex-spouse is missing or uncooperative for the tribunal to declare the person as absent and proceed with the case as long as you can provide other witnesses or documentation. The fact remains, however, that there are some situations in which the tribunal cannot issue a judgment.

> "I was married by a Catholic army chaplain in Vietnam. After I brought my wife to the States, she ran away with a

Vietnamese guy. I have no idea where she is. I heard rumors that she and this guy had been together in Vietnam, and she married me as a ticket to the U.S.A., but I can't prove it. The tribunal says it's a nice story, but how do they know it's true? I have no witnesses, no documentation, and no ex-wife. They told me there is no chance for an annulment." *M.C., New York*

Cases involving foreign brides, migrant workers, multiple marriages, and people advanced in age, who have no living witnesses or access to documentation, often pose problems. Sometimes, after a bitter divorce, an ex-spouse will lie to the tribunal out of spite, and the case becomes deadlocked with one person contradicting the other.

Some people are shocked to learn that the Church recognizes marriages between non-Catholics as valid and requires divorced non-Catholics to seek an annulment of their first marriage before marrying a Catholic.

"My husband is not Catholic and his previous marriage prevents us from being married in the Church. He refuses to apply for a Catholic annulment from his first marriage because both of them were Protestant and married by a Protestant minister. He says the Catholic Church has no business annulling marriages between Protestants." *C.R.J.*

There are other cases where some of the people involved may be physically, psychologically or emotionally incapable of participating in the annulment process.

"I know my first marriage was invalid for several very serious reasons, but in good conscience I could not pursue an annulment because my ex-spouse is psychologically unstable and her therapist told me it would push her and some of her family over the edge. I remarried outside the Church. God will have to be my judge, but I don't believe that in this case God will hold my second marriage against me." *L.B.*

If you know in the depths of your heart that your first marriage was invalid, but there is no possibility of an annulment because of a lack of evidence or some other complicating factor, there might be a possibility of coming back to the Sacraments through what is called the Internal Forum solution. Simply stated, the Internal Forum is the process by which a person arrives at moral certainty that a previous marriage was invalid and knows in the depths of his or her own conscience that the second marriage is a permanent bond in the eyes of God.

This is not a matter of simply saying, "I don't think my first marriage was valid."

The discerning process usually happens during a series of private sessions with a priest. The Internal Forum is considered one of the best kept secrets in the Catholic Church.

"It is a secret because it's not the normal way that we would like to do things," says Msgr. William Gallagher. "The Internal Forum should only be recommended if the couple has already tried the annulment process and failed. It should be an extraordinary means. We don't want people to think there are two separate systems of justice. The tribunal is the normal way to handle these cases. If the tribunal can't, then the Internal Forum is a last ditch effort."

During the process, the priest will probably try to ascertain:

- The reasons why a person considers the first marriage invalid.

- The certainty that the first marriage is completely severed with no possibility of a reconciliation.

- The acceptance of responsibility and repentance for any part the person played in causing the break-up of the marriage.

- The assurance that any obligations to the ex-spouse and children from the marriage will be met.

- The assurance that the new marriage is stable and enduring with a commitment to love, fidelity and care of children.

- A deep desire to receive the Eucharist and become active in the parish community.

- The willingness to avoid scandal by promising not to discuss the situation.

Technically, the priest does not give couples permission to receive Communion, but he can encourage them to follow their consciences. They return to the Sacraments on the condition that "they live according to the demands of Christian moral principles, and that they receive the Sacraments in a church in which they are not known so that they will not create any scandal."

Under no circumstances can a priest conduct a marriage ceremony or a renewal of vows for the couple. It can't be announced to the parish. Depending on the circumstances, the couple may or may not be allowed to serve as a lector, a Eucharistic minister, or a sponsor for Baptism or Confirmation. It is not a perfect solution, and yet for some people, the opportunity to receive Communion and become an active part of a parish community makes it all worthwhile.

"Some of the best volunteers in our parishes have gone through an annulment or an Internal Forum solution," remarks Msgr. Vincent Becker. "These people have thirsted for the Eucharist for so long and with such an intensity that God is up front in their lives. They tend to be more compassionate and less judgmental of others because they have been through so much pain themselves. They give their lives to the Church because they experienced that hunger and thirst, and they are grateful to be back."

Most priests advise couples to hedge if anyone asks specific questions about why they are suddenly receiving Communion. "I usually tell people that if we go through a process of the Internal Forum, don't bring it up again," says Msgr. Becker. "Don't talk about it in confession. Don't discuss it with anyone. It's settled. It is an adult decision you made with a priest looking on from a neutral point of view."

The Church has always recognized the primacy of conscience. From ancient times, the term *epikeia* was used to acknowledge that not every case can be covered by an external law. In the Orthodox Church, a similar concept called *oikonomia* acknowledges that God's mercy surpasses the law.

"We don't want to take away from the dignity of the Sacraments or the teachings of the Church, but we can't forget about these people either," says Father Ron Pecci, OFM. "There are always situations that don't apply to strict interpretations of the law, and the Church has always made allowance for them."

The great fear among some Church officials is that abuses of the Internal Forum will erode the Church's teaching on the indissolubility of marriage and trivialize the Eucharist. Since it is an internal solution, there's no way to gather statistics on it. There's no way to say it's happening a lot or very little.

There are also some cases where people sidestep the whole process and decide on their own without the help of a priest to return to the Sacraments.

> "At my sister's wedding, I was the Maid of Honor and the only member of the wedding party who couldn't receive Communion because I was divorced and remarried. Yes, that hurt. My Dad said, 'You can go if you want to. Just tell them your Father said you could!' I thought that was cute but I couldn't do it. I was too young then, but now I will go to Communion. I have cut out the middle man and made my peace with God directly. I cannot believe God will burn me in hell for wanting to be close to him."
> B.B., *California*

Others make the same decision, but seem less confident in their choice:

"I'm not sure I can live with the unnecessary pain of the annulment process; it feels like punishment, and I haven't done anything wrong. The marriage I'm in now is holy, unlike the first. So I don't think I'm going to get an annulment, but I will participate in the Sacraments until someone stops me. I would prefer a cleaner re-uniting, but I'm afraid to talk to a priest. I'm hurting over this."
M.R.G., Chicago, Illinois

For some, the Internal Forum solution is impossible. "I've talked with people who just cannot believe that the same Church which says a valid marriage lasts forever would permit the Internal Forum," admits Msgr. Becker. "On the other hand, if someone really believes that their first marriage was valid, the Internal Forum is not a possibility."

In many places, priests emphasize the traditional Catholic concept of "Spiritual Communion" for people who cannot receive the Sacraments. Spiritual Communion is a kind of mystical bonding with the Lord when a person is unable to join the community at the Eucharistic table. In the past, the idea of Spiritual Communion served as a link to the community for the sick, the home-bound, children who had not yet made their First Communion, non-Catholics, and people who had broken the Communion fast. The Second Vatican Council reinforced this concept when it emphasized that at Mass the presence of Christ is not limited to the consecrated bread and wine, but is also present in the worshipping community, in the priest, and in the Scripture readings. Today, in some parts of the country, priests will invite anyone in the congregation, who cannot receive the Eucharist to partake in "Spiritual Communion," by approaching the altar in the Communion line, but indicating to the priest that they desire only a special blessing.

"Right now, I feel that I will never receive physical Communion again, but that my life's work will be to learn to receive Spiritual Communion." *C.R.J.*

Another traditional option is the practice of admitting to the Sacraments divorced and remarried couples who agree to live together as brother and sister. It is not a practical solution for some couples.

> "If I tell my husband we cannot live as man and wife, he will be out the door in less than five minutes. He is the only father my children have ever known. Is this what God wants?" *S.M.L.*

While the prospect is unthinkable for some, it is a viable solution for others, including Danielle and Maurice Bourgeois of Quebec. Danielle was divorced when she met Maurice. After 15 years together, they underwent a spiritual conversion which led them to start a group called Myriam-Solitude for divorced men and women who consecrate themselves to God with a promise of celibacy. Since 1986, the group has grown to over 300 members.

"Some people say, 'Maurice and Danielle are out of their minds,'" admits Danielle Bourgeois. "Yes, but we are extremely happy! We know a much greater happiness than the happiness we had before as a couple. Our consecration doesn't make of us religious. We remain lay people... We remain fathers and mothers. Someday we will be grandparents. We do have a family duty to fill out. We don't leave the family. This is, for us, our ministry within the Sacrament of Marriage."

For many couples the only other alternative is joining a Protestant Church. A Lutheran minister in upstate New York jokingly claims that he prays every morning that the Catholic Church will never change its stand on divorce and remarriage because some of his best church leaders are fallen-away Catholics, who would return to the Catholic Church in an instant if the rules were changed. His little joke always gets a big laugh, but there's a lot of truth in it.

> "It has been two years since we began the annulment process and we have yet to hear from the diocese about

anything. My husband and I finally got married in a
Lutheran Church and we couldn't have asked for a more
perfect wedding. The Lutheran Church was so much
easier, kinder and more personal. These are all things that
I found lacking in my dealings with the Catholic Church
throughout my entire life. But I still feel it necessary to
raise my children (when we have them) Catholic. This is
the main reason I would like to complete the annulment
process." *Theresa Gothard, Fairfax, Virginia*

"I am always embarrassed when I meet with ecumenical
clergy because I know that they are doing part of my work,"
admits Msgr. William Gallagher. "They perform marriages for
sincere convicted Catholic Christians, who cannot be married
in the Catholic Church because their annulments haven't come
through. These ministers will say, 'I did two of your weddings
this weekend.' They take these couples on knowing that if the
annulment papers come through, the couple will come back to
the Catholic Church. I feel terrible, but I can't fix it."

Sometimes, couples leave the Catholic Church and stay
away.

"After several years of not attending any church, I became
terribly depressed especially at Easter and Christmas. I
decided that if the Catholic Church would not accept us,
we would go to some other Church. We started attending
a Baptist Church, and put our children in bible study
classes." *P.G.*

"My husband and I tried to stick with the Catholic
Church, but when our oldest child reached the age of First
Communion, we couldn't stand the thought of not being
able to receive Communion as a family, so we switched to
an Episcopalian Church. Now, at least, we can all participate fully." *L.K.*

"We have found peace and a sense of belonging as
Lutherans. I know in my heart that God accepts our

marriage even if the Catholic Church does not. God knows what is in our hearts and he is the only one that can decide the fate of our souls." *N.C.*

While divorce and remarriage is one of the biggest stumbling blocks for Catholics, it is not the only one. In the next chapter, we'll look at some of the other reasons people question whether there's a place for them in the Catholic Church.

Chapter Notes

"The Church, which was set up to lead to salvation...": Pope John Paul II, *Familiaris Consortio*, 84.e. Divorced persons who have remarried, 1981.

"cannot be admitted to the Eucharist..." *Ibid.*

"they live according to the demands of Christian moral principles...": John M. Huels, OFM, *The Pastoral Companion: A Canon Law Handbook for Catholic Ministry*, Chicago: Franciscan Herald Press, p. 260, SCDF, letter of March 21, 1975, CLD 9:504-5.

The Second Vatican Council reinforced this concept...": Vatican II, "Constitution on the Sacred Liturgy."

CHAPTER 16

Is There a Place for Me in the Catholic Church?

"I left the Catholic Church for many reasons, but mostly because I am gay and could not find a parish that would accept me." *J.W.*

"I believe women should be able to become priests. I believe it is the Catholic organization, not God or Jesus, that keeps women in their current roles. I resent all the guilt the Church has put on me if I don't do this or think that. I resent the way I'm treated like a second class citizen." *D.H.*

"I was told that since I disagreed with some of the Church's teachings, I was not a Catholic and should leave. I was also told there was nowhere here to get help. Is this what the Church wants? Is there no help? I still find peace in the Church, but I am afraid the Church finds no peace in me." *K.McH.*

"It's hard to express how unwelcoming the Catholic Church feels sometimes." *C.R.*

On Sunday mornings in Nacogdoches, Texas, six women gather in Meg Gloger's living room to pray. A former nun, Ms. Gloger felt called to ministry, and in 1992, she graduated from

Chicago's Loyola University with a degree in divinity. With no hope of being ordained in the Catholic Church, she returned to Texas and started her own "woman-church."

"I just cannot abide the Church's attitude toward women any more," she says. "We are excluded by sexist language and symbolism, negated as individuals and only valued for our labor and our mothering abilities…"

In St. Louis, Helen Hull Hitchcock, executive director of the traditionalist group, Women for Faith and Family, called Ms. Gloger's woman-church nothing more than "loopy New Age stuff."

"Why do they feel the need to invent a new religion?" she asked. "What they're doing is rejecting the whole Judeo-Christian religion sweepingly, and they're not willing to adopt any other non-Christian or non-Jewish religion."

At sessions for returning Catholics, women's issues always emerge as one of the toughest topics. Equally difficult are issues related to the Church teachings on gays and lesbians. Here are some of the questions raised:

- **Why can't women be ordained?**

In his May, 1994, encyclical *Ordinatio sacerdotalis*, Pope John Paul II stated unequivocally that the Church has "no authority whatsoever to confer priestly ordination on women." He substantiates his point in part on the basis that Jesus chose only men as his apostles. Since Jesus often moved against the cultural mores of the times, the fact that he did not choose women when he could have is an indication to the Pope that only men should be ordained to the priesthood.

In the wake of this encyclical, theologians and Catholic feminists debated the Pope's position. In November, 1995, the Sacred Congregation for the Doctrine of the Faith issued a statement reaffirming the Pope's teaching that the Church has no authority to ordain women, and stated that there should be no further discussion on this point. Several prominent and highly respected theologians even went so far as to say that the way in which the document was worded put it in the category of an infallibly defined article of faith. Others disagreed.

In spite of all of this, you will find that many Catholic women (and men, for that matter) continue to struggle over this issue. Some Catholic women agree totally with the Pope; some question the position but are not willing to stick their necks out; some simply don't care one way or the other; some are still willing to fight; some give up and leave the Church.

This issue is especially difficult for women who believe in their hearts that they are called to the priesthood. Some of them leave in good conscience to pursue ordination in another church. Others stay and try to work for God in a restricted capacity within the Catholic Church.

- **Why doesn't the Church recognize God as both genders, instead of neither gender?**

The new *Catechism of the Catholic Church* explains: "In no way is God in man's image. God is neither man nor woman. God is pure spirit in which there is no place for the differences between the sexes."

- **Why is it that the Catholic Church doesn't believe in gender equality?**

The Church teachings on the roles of men and women are based on the idea of complementarity, meaning men and women are equally loved by God, but they were created to work together, not in competition, with separate, but equally important responsibilities.

- **What is the current Church position on gays and lesbians?**

In the past, the Church condemned homosexuality as "an intrinsic moral disorder." Today, the Church recognizes that a homosexual orientation is not a matter of choice, and insists that gays and lesbians "must be accepted with respect, compassion, and sensitivity." However, because the Church teachings on sexuality are based on the requirement that every act of sexual expression must be open to the possibility of new life, all sexual acts outside of marriage — both heterosexual and homosexual — are considered wrong. As a result, the official Church teaching is that gays and lesbians are "called to chastity."

- **What is the current opinion and practice of the Catholic Church on the issue of gay and lesbian couples as permanent life-partners?**

In a statement issued July 24, 1996, the U.S. Catholic bishops opposed granting the legal status of marriage to a relationship between persons of the same sex.

- **I'm gay, but I'm not currently in a relationship with anyone. Can I receive Communion?**

Yes.

- **What is the position of the Church on the ordination of gay men?**

Each diocese forms its own policy on ordination. Since priests take vows of chastity at ordination and are expected to live a celibate life, there is no universal policy on the sexual orientation of priests.

- **I keep hearing about how accepting the Church is of gays and lesbians, but it doesn't feel that way to me. Is there a place for gays and lesbians in the Church?**

Most dioceses have special ministries for gays and lesbians. The National Association of Catholic Diocesan Lesbian and Gay Ministries (NACDLGM) has a listing of what is available nationwide. For information, call 510-465-9344 or e-mail NACDLGM@aol.com. They are located at 433 Jefferson Street, Oakland, California 94607.

You can also call your Chancery or contact the Newman Center at the closest college or university, and ask what kind of programs are available in your area.

• **If a priest suspected that my housemate and I had a lesbian relationship, could he publicly refuse to give us Communion?**

No.

• **What is the difference between Dignity and Courage?**

Dignity is an independent national organization of gay and lesbian Catholics, which is not officially recognized by the Church because it does not promote sexual abstinence among its members. Courage is an organization for gay and lesbian Catholics, which is recognized in some dioceses because it promotes chastity, and uses the 12-step program to help members refrain from sexual activity.

Part of the difficulty raised by these kinds of questions is that the answers always seem like black and white, dogmatic responses which sound harsh and uncaring.

"The painful reality of this ministry lies in the fact that the Church's official stance is often what Bishop Kenneth Untener of Saginaw, Michigan, referred to as 'corporate severity,'" observed Carrie Kemp and Father Don Pologruto, who began organizing programs for inactive Catholics in 1984. "The bishop qualified his concerns by stating, 'I believe that Church ministers, when dealing one-to-one with people, generally tend to be very compassionate.'"

At most Come Home programs, people struggling with these kinds of issues are urged to speak privately with a priest. For people who want to deal with these issues in an open forum, this is unacceptable. For others, it is a first step that often leads to healing and a peaceful resolution of their concerns.

Sister Irene Nerney, RSM, resolved her struggle with women's issues when she came to the realization that her situation could make her or break her. "I decided I was not going to become a bitter, angry woman," she said, "because if I did that, I would not be able to do good."

For others, the question of whether or not they can be part of the Church is less clear:

> "I feel uncertain whether the Church is a healthy place for a gay man struggling with his own self-esteem. I don't know if I could ever come back. I would need to find a parish where I felt as if I was really accepted for who I am." *D.T.*

"It is also important to remember that healing does not always mean a return to active participation in the Catholic Church," observe Carrie Kemp and Father Don Pologruto. "For some the pain is so intense that the best we can hope for is a healing of their scars, a healing that cannot take place if they return to the Church. While they feel that it is safer to live with healed wounds outside of the Church, they may acknowledge and express appreciation for the healing that has taken place and the fellowship that provided the framework for that healing. But their journey teaches them not to pursue any further reconnection with the Church. And so they move on, stronger and more at peace with their God. They go with our friendship and our blessings."

Only you can answer the question: "Is there a place for me in the Catholic Church?" Before you answer, however, take some time to investigate your options, examine your conscience, and listen to God speaking in the depths of your soul. Then do what you believe is right.

> "When I die, I don't think God will ask me if I was Catholic. I think God will ask me to account for my life in general." *M.G.*

> "I chose to remain Catholic because I consider my religion to be a personal relationship with God, and I am abso-

lutely confident that the Lord does not think less of me as a woman or as a lesbian." *A.B.N.*

"My attempts to return have not been easy. If it wasn't for my faith that God can do anything and that God is not so hung up on the legalistics of religion, I don't know what I would do. I only hope He gives me patience to work through what the Church has become. I regularly check in with Him when things start to frustrate me through prayer and meditation — and He says not to worry. For those of us who are coming home, keep true to what God tells you, and if some set of rules or opinions don't feel right, keep looking, keep knocking around. There is great diversity here, but sometimes it gets lost behind all the rest." *Eilish Maura*

Chapter Notes

On Sunday mornings in Nacogdoches, Texas…: Deborah Caldwell, "In God, Women Trust," *Buffalo News*, April 26, 1996, p. C-11.

"Why do they feel the need…": *Ibid.*, p. C-12.

"In no way is God in man's image…": CCC, # 370.

"must be accepted with respect, compassion, and sensitivity.": CCC, # 2357, 2358.

"called to chastity." CCC, # 2359.

"I decided I was not going to become…": Linda Borg, "For Catholics, Questions of Obedience," *Buffalo News*, July 13, 1996, p. C-7.

"The painful reality of this ministry…": Carrie Kemp and Donald Pologruto, *Catholics Coming Home: A Handbook for Churches Reaching Out to Inactive Catholics*, Harper San Francisco: 1990, p. 121

"It is also important to remember…": *Ibid.*, p. 22.

CHAPTER 17

The Question Box

At most Come Home sessions, a question box is available for people who may not feel comfortable asking a question in an open forum. Here are some of the questions participants have submitted over the years:

- **Someone told me that I am automatically excommunicated once my divorce is final. Someone else told me that is not true and I am still a Catholic in good standing. Who is right?**

A divorced person is NOT automatically excommunicated. Divorce is not a sin. As long as you have not committed any other serious sins, you are still in good standing with the Church and can continue to receive Communion.

- **Are you automatically excommunicated if you are divorced and remarry outside the Church?**

No. In May, 1977, the National Conference of Catholic Bishops removed the penalty of excommunication imposed by the Third Plenary Council of Baltimore (1884) on American Catholics who divorced and remarried.

- **If I have had an abortion, how do I ask God for forgiveness and get back into the Catholic Church?**

You can receive God's healing forgiveness in the Sacrament of Reconciliation.

- **Can I be pro-choice (regarding abortion) and be a practicing Roman Catholic?**

  What do you mean by pro-choice? The Church teaches that abortion is objectively wrong. While the moral issues are pretty clear, there are some legal concerns which fall into a somewhat grayer area. There are some practicing Catholics — mainly law enforcement officials and judges, for example — who are required by their oath of office to uphold the law of the land which permits abortion. There are also Catholic legislators and politicians, who personally oppose abortion, but do not believe that a government in a democratic society has a right to ban abortion if the majority of the people believe abortion should be permitted. Perhaps you should discuss this further with a priest.

- **Can someone who has had a vasectomy or a tubal ligation still be a Catholic?**

  Yes.

- **If I confessed that I underwent surgical sterilization as a permanent method of birth control, would the priest tell me to have the procedure surgically reversed before I could receive absolution?**

  No.

- **Would a voluntary vasectomy (performed because my wife has several chronic medical problems which could be dangerous if she became pregnant) be a detriment to obtaining an annulment?**

  No.

- **I know I am in a serious state of sin, but I don't feel comfortable discussing my situation with a local priest. Can I go to a priest that I don't know in another town?**

  Yes.

• **I was away from the Church for 15 years, and when I decided to come back I went to Confession.** I told the priest I was baptized and received my First Communion, but I haven't been confirmed. He told me to join the parish RCIA program. The nun in charge of RCIA told me that I have to stop receiving Communion until after I am confirmed. Is this true? I came back to the Church because of the Eucharist and I can't bear to give it up again.

There is no reason why you should be prohibited from receiving Communion. Talk to the priest in your parish and try to straighten this out.

• **Do Catholics still believe in limbo?**

The Church teaching about limbo began after St. Augustine (354-430) maintained that a soul could not enter heaven without Baptism. Questions arose as to what happens to babies who die without Baptism or to people who die without ever having heard of Jesus Christ. In an attempt to reconcile God's love and mercy with this teaching on Baptism, theologians created limbo — not as a doctrine or as a matter of faith — but as a theological supposition which suggested that limbo was a place of natural happiness like heaven, but without the presence of God. Today, the Church entrusts anyone who dies without Baptism to the great love and mercy of God.

• **Do Catholics still believe that only Catholics can go to heaven?**

No. "Those who, through no fault of their own, do not know the Gospel of Christ or his Church, but who nevertheless seek God with a sincere heart, and, moved by grace, try in their actions to do his will as they know it through the dictates of their conscience — those, too, may achieve eternal salvation." [Vatican II Document, *Lumen Gentium*, 16.]

• **Why did they change the rule about not eating meat on Friday?**

A lot of the rules and regulations of the Pre-Vatican II Church began as reminders of our need to do penance for our own sins and the sins of the world and to detach ourselves from the material goods and pleasures of this life to more actively focus on God and our eternal home with him. Reminders became rules; rules carried sanctions, and sanctions created fear of reprisal (hell fire and damnation, even!) should the rules be broken. And the whole purpose of the practice got lost. There had to be a better way — other practices which would accomplish the same thing while keeping the focus on the original purpose behind the rule. Hence, during Vatican II the old laws were abolished and replaced with the suggestion that each individual determine what kind of penance would best contribute to his or her own spiritual growth. Many Catholics continue to abstain from meat on Friday with precisely this new attitude and outlook in mind.

• **Why doesn't the Catholic Church promote reading of Scripture?**

The Catholic Church does promote the reading of Scripture both individually and in liturgy as a source of prayer and nourishment for a Christian life. Many parishes offer adult Bible study classes, and Scripture is an important element in religious education programs for Catholic children.

• **Does the Church teach you not to question the Church's views?**

Yes and no. The unchanging doctrinal beliefs of the Catholic Church are contained principally in Scripture, the Apostles Creed, the Nicene Creed and the documents of the Church formulated in various ecumenical councils. The Church also expects Catholics to take seriously its moral teachings on human rights and social justice. Questioning the Church's views is often a way of deepening your understanding of them. The Church also recognizes that a well-formed conscience plays a very important role. One of the documents from Vatican II states: "Every man has the duty, and therefore the right, to seek the truth in matters religious in order that he may with prudence form for himself right and true judgment of conscience... [T]he enquiry is to be free, carried on with the aid of teaching or instruction, communication and dialogue. On his part, man perceives and acknowledges the imperatives of the divine law through the mediation of conscience. In all his activity a man is bound to follow his conscience faithfully, in order that he may come to God, for whom he was created. It follows that he is not to be forced to act in a manner contrary to his conscience. Nor, on the other hand, is he to be restrained from acting in accordance with his conscience especially in matters religious." [Vatican II, *Declaration on Religious Freedom*, 3]

- **Do any diocesan priests take vows of poverty as most orders of women religious do?**

    Most diocesan priests take promises of chastity and obedience. There are, however, some diocesan priests who take voluntary vows of poverty in an attempt to live out the evangelical counsels.

- **When are priests going to be allowed to marry?**

    We already have married priests in the Catholic Church. In the Eastern Rites, men are allowed to marry before ordination. There are also married Anglican and Lutheran ministers, who converted to Catholicism and were allowed to become Catholic priests. Currently, there are more than 50 such married priests throughout the United States. The issue of celibacy in the Roman Catholic priesthood is a Church law, not a divine law, and, hence, it could be changed at some point in the future.

• **Why does the Church have to establish a retirement fund for the religious? Couldn't the Church create annuities for them as other employers do?**

Religious priests, brothers and sisters are not Church employees. Their religious communities are canonically erected by the Church, but are expected to be self-supporting. In the past, younger members helped to support the older ones and little thought was given to such things as retirement funds and other kinds of insurance for old age. Now, with the decline in religious vocations, some religious orders find it difficult to support increasing numbers of old and infirm members. The retirement fund was established in gratitude for the service of these dedicated people who worked over the years for little or no salary and had made no provisions for their own retirement. The fund insures that elderly and sick religious will receive the care they deserve. It is completely voluntary for Catholics as to whether or not to contribute.

• **In the eyes of God are you considered a good Catholic if you do not attend Mass every week?**

Some Catholics might say that you're not a good Catholic if you don't participate in the weekly celebration of the Eucharist, but no one can tell you what God would say. God is love, so if we imagine God as a close, personal friend, who loves you very much, it might clarify this a little. Let's suppose that your friend waited for you every week to come and visit. Sometimes you showed up, and sometimes you didn't. Your friend might understand that you have a good reason for not coming, and would still love you, but would probably miss you and long for your presence. When you did show up, your friend would be filled with joy. God's love is like that. It is infinite and unchanging. God loves us even when we don't return that love. When you think of Mass as a celebration of God's love instead of an obligation, it sometimes changes your perspective.

• **Does watching Mass on television count?**

If you're sick and can't get to church, then television Masses are better than nothing, but when you're watching the priest on a screen, you really aren't participating in the liturgy in the fullest sense. You are not physically present with the worshipping community, and you cannot partake of the Eucharistic banquet.

• **I was a Godparent when I was still in good standing in the Church. Now I'm divorced and remarried and can no longer be a Godparent. What about my first Godparent responsibility?**

Your responsibility as a Godparent does not change.

• **How does a divorced non-Catholic get into the Church?**

A divorced non-Catholic would enter the Church through the Rite of Christian Initiation for Adults (RCIA).

• **Do I have to join the parish closest to my residence?**

No. You can belong to any parish you choose. Often, though not always, you will find the one closest to your residence to be the most convenient for you and for the priests who will be serving your spiritual needs. Since certain functions are performed and records kept in one's parish (Baptism, Confirmation, Marriage, Funerals, etc.), it is important that you be registered *somewhere* as a parishioner.

• **I was denied a Church annulment 15 years ago. Can I try again?**

Yes.

• **My husband left me for another woman. Can he have our marriage annulled and marry his girlfriend in the Catholic Church?**

He can apply for an annulment, but it would only be granted if there were sufficient evidence to prove that there was not valid consent at the time your marriage vows were exchanged.

- **The marriage tribunal told me that they were placing a "vetitum" on my case. What does that mean?**

It means that you will not be allowed to marry again in the Catholic Church unless certain conditions are met. For example, if the annulment was granted on psychological grounds, you may be required to undergo a psychological examination to make sure that you are capable of entering into a new marriage commitment.

- **Can a priest refuse to marry a couple who have been living together?**

A priest can refuse to marry a couple if he believes there is some impediment to a valid exchange of vows.

- **How can we take instruction from the Pope when he is so wealthy yet takes a vow of poverty? He is so important in this religion, yet this hypocrisy takes away all his credibility.**

Only order priests, like Franciscans, take vows of poverty. The Pope was ordained a diocesan priest, and therefore took only vows of chastity and obedience, so technically there is no hypocrisy. Your question about poverty has been posed for centuries, however, and is a challenge not just for the clergy, but for each of us as Christians in trying to live the Gospel message. We are all called to poverty of spirit and generosity. In all fairness, we have to say that the present Pope, surrounded as he is with all the pomp and splendor of the Vatican, still lives a pretty austere lifestyle of hard work and a busy schedule.

- **The Church considers my second marriage invalid, but we** still want to raise our children Catholic. **Is it true that a priest will not baptize our children unless we obtain an annulment?**

No. It is not true. You may register in a parish and raise your children in the Catholic faith. If a particular pastor gives you a hard time, go to another parish.

- **Can a priest refuse to baptize my baby because I'm not married to the baby's father?**

No. Canon 868 states that for the baptism of an infant it is necessary that:

1. the parents or at least one of them or the person who lawfully takes their place gives consent;

2. there be a founded hope that the infant will be brought up in the Catholic religion.

- **My mother told my Protestant fiancé that before we can be married in a Catholic church, he has to sign a paper saying that he promises to raise our children Catholic. Is this true?**

No. Canon law no longer requires a non-Catholic to sign a promise to raise the children Catholic. A dispensation, however, is required for the marriage and the Catholic must promise that he or she will make a sincere effort to raise the children Catholic.

- **Is it true that the Church now allows Catholics to be cremated?**

Yes.

- **Our local priest refused to bury my neighbor, who was a fallen-away Catholic. One of the relatives in the family got mad and called the Chancery. A funeral was arranged in another parish. What's the story? Can a priest refuse to bury someone?**

This question always comes up when a person who has been away from the Church for many years dies, and some priest refuses Christian burial. On the other end of town, another priest says, "I'll do the funeral because it's a moment of grace for the whole family." These conflicting views are due to different interpretations of Canon law.

Technically, Canon 1184 states that unless a person has given some signs of repentance before death, a priest can refuse ecclesiastical funeral rites for:

1. notorious apostates, heretics and schismatics;
2. persons who had chosen the cremation of their own bodies for reasons opposed to the Christian faith;
3. other manifest sinners for whom ecclesiastical funeral rites cannot be granted without public scandal to the faithful.

Most fallen-away Catholics would not fit into these categories. Canon law also states that if some doubt should arise, the local bishop should be consulted.

- **Is it true that you cannot have a Catholic funeral if you are divorced?**

    No. It is not true.

- **Can you be buried in a Catholic cemetery if you are divorced?**

    Yes.

- **Can someone who committed suicide have a Catholic funeral and be buried in a Catholic cemetery?**

    Yes.

- **Can a non-Catholic husband be buried next to his Catholic wife in a Catholic cemetery?**

    Yes.

- **Can a Protestant, who married a Catholic and attended Mass throughout his life, although he never converted, have a Catholic funeral?**

Yes. Canon 1183 states: "In the prudent judgment of the local ordinary, ecclesiastical funeral rites can be granted to baptized members of some non-Catholic church or ecclesial community unless it is evidently contrary to their will and provided their own minister is unavailable."

- **Suppose I have found a wonderful minister in another religion. If I come back to the Catholic Church I would not want to cut off that friendship and religious experience. Any comments?**

Lots of Catholics maintain friendships with people of other faiths. There's no need to cut off your relationship with this minister if you decide to return to Catholicism. While it would be impossible to practice both religions, you could certainly engage in the social activities in both churches.

- **If I came back to the Catholic Church would I have to give up my membership with the Masons?**

In the United States, many people argue that the Masons are a philanthropic organization and there is no danger to the faith of Catholics. In parts of Europe, however, the Masons are still vehemently anti-Catholic. The prohibition from belonging to the Masons was removed from the Code of Canon Law in the 1983 revisions. However, that same year, the Sacred Congregation for the Doctrine of Faith reinforced the ban on Catholics becoming Masons because "the stated goals of Freemasonry remain incompatible with the Gospel of Christ and the teaching of the Catholic Church." You may want to discuss this with your parish priest.

CHAPTER 18

Finding the Right Priest

"I would like to speak to a priest, but I'm afraid I will be rejected. Should I just call the nearest church or go there?" *A.M.*

"There are priests who have some distasteful qualities. What bothers me the most about them is not that they don't have a clue, it's that they don't seem to care about people." *R.D.*

"What do you do when one priest tells you something and another priest tells you the opposite?" *T.R.*

When psychologist and writer, Sidney Callahan decided to become Catholic in 1953, she went to St. Matthew's Cathedral in Washington, D.C., and found herself arguing with the priest on duty:

> I told him I came there because the local priest in Bryn Mawr refused to have anything to do with Bryn Mawr girls. Furthermore, I hated the ornate decorations of St. Matthew's and knew that Joe McCarthy went there. My line was that if I could enter the Catholic Church there, at the bottom so to speak, I could always manage anywhere else.
> This priest turned out to be McCarthy's great friend and

spiritual advisor, so no wonder we had a total non-meeting of the minds. He quickly decided to turn me over to a delightful old French priest in residence, "another heretic like you." This priest had spent his life in the missions in India and was spiritual, worldly, and wise as well as kind and witty. We agreed on everything, from a devotion to the Spirit to a dismissal of the Index and the various legalisms which used to vex Catholics in those days. We zoomed through instruction since I'd already read myself into Roman Catholicism à la Newman, and I was received into the Church with a great deal of inner joy.

Finding a priest is an important element in the process of coming back to the Church, but unfortunately there are no magic formulas or simple steps to follow.

For someone like Sidney Callahan, assertively standing her ground until she found a priest who could respond to her intellectual and spiritual needs proved to be the right method.

For others, the anonymity of the confessional with an unknown priest on the other side of the screen is the answer. Father John Catoir, who heard confessions at St. Patrick's Cathedral in New York City for five years, notes that many tourists and business people from out of town would come into the confessional on an impulse and begin their journey back to the Church after a lapse of 10 or 20 years.

Some people might find the idea of walking into a confessional to an unknown priest too threatening, however. They may feel uncomfortable going into a dark, confined space. They may fear that their confession will take too long, and other people in line will be irritated. They may harbor childhood memories of people overhearing priests scolding other people in the confessional, or they may have been scolded themselves.

What many Catholics don't realize is that Canon law upholds your freedom to select a priest. Father James Lee Dugan, SJ, stuns Come Home audiences with stories of Europeans who encounter a difficult priest in the confessional and simply walk out with the casual statement, "I'm sorry you're having such a bad day, Father." Then, they try another priest in a different confessional.

It takes a lot of courage to walk out of a confessional and try again, especially for someone who is struggling with deep-seated pain, fear, uncertainty or feelings of rejection.

> "Perhaps if any of you priests out there could read some of this, you might know that we are not just railing against the Church or the circumstances that brought us here, but that we feel a true calling to union within the Church and you separate us from it by law and by cruelty, intended or not, and by sometimes simply not attending to the needs of the seekers who come to your doors. I wish there was a more concerted, kind effort to effect reconciliations to the Church. Meanwhile, I keep praying for the clarity and the strength I need." *C.R.J.*

Father Flavian Walsh urges people to shop around for a priest. "When you are going to go to a dentist or a doctor would you just walk off the street into any office?" he asks. "Wouldn't you ask other people for referrals? Well, you should do the same thing when you're looking for spiritual guidance."

If the idea of shopping around for a priest seems completely alien, you're not alone. "All priests should be kind and understanding," many participants at Come Home programs protest. "All priests should care about people."

Technically, that's true. But since human strengths and weaknesses, temperaments, age, illness and personalities are uncontrollable factors, it's also true that some priests will meet your intellectual, emotional and spiritual needs better than others.

Father Gary Bagley believes there are two vastly different types of people in most Come Home sessions, and these people look for completely different traits in a priest. "Some folks want to be led back to the Church," he explains.

When you start talking about finding your way back, they almost feel helpless. They want a priest to take them by the hand. They are genuinely hurting people, who need to be guided back. I don't think I'm good at that.

I'm better with the folks on the opposite end of the spectrum, who left the Church because they didn't want to be over-directed, and they don't want to be over-directed coming back, either. They want to wrestle with the questions and struggle with their anger and frustration in an attempt to find their own way back. I am much better at working with them.

Think for a moment about what you want from a priest: Are you looking for a kind, gentle, father-image who will soothe and comfort you? Or do you want an intellectual-type who will debate issues and challenge you? Do you want someone who can counsel you? Maybe you just need someone to answer your questions. Maybe you want advice or reassurance. Maybe you want someone who will pray with you. Maybe you want someone who will listen. Maybe you're not sure what you want.

"I went to see a priest because I had questions about the annulment process, but he was so patient and understanding that I ended up pouring out my whole messy life to him. At the end he told me that without realizing it, I had just made a general confession, and he gave me absolution for all the sins of my life." *C.L.D., Michigan*

Most parishes that advertise programs for returning Catholics have built-in referral systems to connect people with priests. Some programs offer participants a list of priests who specialize in different areas such as annulments, or counseling, or spiritual healing.

"One gay man told me that he went to confession and the priest was mean and didn't understand gay issues," Father

Flavian recalls. "I gave him ten names and told him, 'Call one of these priests and make an appointment.'"

If you live in a large metropolitan area, shopping for a priest can be as simple as attending Mass in different parishes, watching the priests, and listening to their homilies until you find one that seems to be approachable.

For people who live in small towns or in areas where there are few Catholics and no organized programs for returning Catholics, finding a priest can be a little more challenging, especially if you're hesitant about talking to someone in your local parish. If you're simply looking for answers or advice and you have access to the Internet, you'll find priests on the Catholic message boards who can answer your questions. But even on the Internet, you'll find that priests have different personalities and different points of view.

When you get conflicting advice from two different priests, it can be alarming and confusing. Try to put it into the same perspective that you would if you got differing medical opinions from two different doctors. It simply means that you have to continue your search and seek out other opinions.

Father Joe Rogliano suggests that priestly advice can vary because priests might come from different schools of thought or might have received different training in the seminary: "Sometimes the conflicting views come from different interpretations of Church law."

Father William McKee, CSSR, agrees: "A problem many of us older priests have is that our education was largely a head trip. Reason, logic, objectivity, doctrine, dogma, and law. Very little was taught about the validity of emotions and feelings."

If you're looking for a priest to talk to and you don't have any personal referrals, Father John Catoir suggests that you make some phone calls to rectories in different parts of the city or in nearby towns. "Ask to speak to a priest and tell him that you want to come back to the Church. If he sounds open, kind and understanding, make an appointment. If not, hang up and try again."

"I called the rectory office and talked to the secretary. I figured she would know which priest would be the most approachable. I told her I wanted to come back to the Church, and I needed to talk to a priest. She told me exactly who to see and who to stay away from." *W.K.T.*

You can also call the diocesan offices and ask for names of priests who specialize in different areas such as family life, young adults, teens, annulments, spiritual direction, or gay and lesbian ministry. The key is not to get discouraged if things don't work out with the first priest you call.

"I called the rectory closest to my home. The priest wasn't in. I left a message on the answering machine. It wasn't returned. I called another rectory, the second closest to home. I told the pastor that I was interested in making an appointment to discuss my return to the Church. It seemed as though it would be okay. I had two more sessions with this priest and then something went wrong. To this day I do not know what caused it, but he started to shun me in church. I thought at first that he was busy with others but slowly I began to see it was real. I couldn't ask him about it because he wouldn't talk to me. This caused me a great deal of pain. I have since found another priest that I can talk to." *C.S., New York*

Most priests will try to help you, and if they can't, they will refer you to someone who can. If you have a bad experience, chalk it off to human nature.

"Some priests are jerks and some priests are wonderful. That's life." *L.A.*

Ultimately, it's up to you to take the initiative in finding the right priest, and that means overcoming whatever negative feelings or fears you might have. If you really believe that God is leading you back to the Church, pray for guidance. Remember Jesus' promise: "Ask and it will be given to you; seek and you will find; knock and the door will be opened to you. For everyone who asks, receives; and to the one who knocks, the door will be opened" (Mt 7:7-8).

"I was told by two different priests at two churches in my area that I could not have my children baptized until I took care of my marriage annulment. At that time I barely had money to survive. After several years of searching other churches, I went back to the Catholic Church and a younger priest told me right off that he would help me get the children baptized. That seems to be the feeling among priests now, that they will listen and help you to do what's right. My kids and I have returned to the Church, and I have never been happier." *P.G.L.*

"I sat down with a priest, and before I knew it, I was crying. I kept saying that I just wanted to come home, but I was scared because of all my questions. Father listened with the patience of Job. He told me that I wasn't alone in my questioning and he reminded me that the only way to have questions answered is to ask them. He encouraged me to study and learn more. He also told me that for my penance, I would have to do something to get involved. I liked to sing, so joining the choir was natural. I also began to read books about the Catholic faith, some which were authorized by the Church and some of which weren't. I asked my questions and I learned that I had always believed in the things I had challenged. I just needed an outlet to voice my doubts. I learned to ask questions in a constructive, not a destructive way. I learned to support the Church again in her efforts to discover and to teach the truth, even if I don't always agree with the manner in which it teaches." *Julie Richard, Kansas City, Missouri*

Chapter Notes

"I told him I came there because the local priest...": John J. Delaney, Editor, *Why Catholic?*, New York: Doubleday & Company, Inc., 1979, pp. 23-24.

Canon law upholds your freedom...: Code of Canon Law, canon 991.

CHAPTER 19

Bless me Father, for I have sinned...

"I've been away from the Church for many years. I do not remember the words used in confession. I remember the phrase, 'Bless me, Father, for I have sinned.' Is this phrase still used and what comes next?" *D.M.G., Pennsylvania*

"When I was a teenager, I confessed that I found some *Playboy* magazines. The priest yelled so loud that everyone in the church heard him. I haven't been to confession since." *R.H.*

"I am in a 12-step program, and we confess to one another. That keeps me sane and on the right track but I've found myself wondering if confession with a priest gives you an impartial person's view. If I come back to the Church, do I have to go to confession?" *J.L.*

While every religion talks about guilt, sin and forgiveness, Catholicism is the only religion that sacramentalizes it. The idea should be a comforting one, yet the mere mention of the word confession at Come Home sessions evokes fear, anger, shame, confusion, guilt, embarrassment, anxiety and intense curiosity. Almost every person has a confession horror story that happened to themselves or to someone they know. The stories are almost never humorous. Likewise, almost everyone has a question or two about the sacrament. For example:

- **Why should I go to confession if I have my own talks with God?**

You can have your own talks with God, and if you are sincerely sorry, God will forgive you. Scripture also says, "Confess your sins to one another," so if you are in a support group where you openly admit your character flaws and weaknesses, God will forgive you. In fact, bartenders and beauticians probably hear more confessions than many priests do. There are, however, several special advantages that the Sacrament of Reconciliation offers that these others can't provide. First, there is the assurance that through the power of Jesus Christ, the priest has the power to absolve your sins, and through this absolution you have the assurance of God's forgiving love and the full acceptance of the Church community. No questions. No doubts. You are forgiven. You also receive the special grace of the sacrament which helps you move from imperfect to perfect contrition.

- **I've heard that some places have communal penance services with general absolution. Is that true?**

It is true that priests can celebrate communal penance services with general absolution, but the conditions are very limited. Canon 961 states that a priest can give general absolution when a large number of people are in danger of death, such as on an airplane about to crash or a ship about to sink. General absolution can also be used when there are not enough priests to hear a large number of individual confessions, but a person who has serious sins remitted through general absolution should confess those sins to a priest at the first opportunity.

- **Is there still a distinction between venial and mortal sins?**

Mortal sin is "a grave violation of God's law" that turns a person away from God. For a sin to be mortal, it must be a serious matter, you must know that it is serious, and you must give full consent to it.

Venial sin is a less serious offense which "does not deprive the person of sanctifying grace, friendship with God, charity, and consequently eternal happiness."

- **I know priests aren't suppose to tell what they hear in the confessional, but what if you did something illegal? Are there any circumstances where a priest could testify against you?**

No. Canon law states that "the sacramental seal is inviolable; therefore, it is a crime for a confessor in any way to betray a penitent by word or in any other manner or for any reason."

- **What happens to a priest who breaks the seal of the confessional?**

A priest who breaks the seal of the confessional incurs automatic excommunication, but there are no known cases of this ever happening.

- **I was sexually involved with someone but I'm afraid to go to confession because I don't want to reveal the person's identity.**

You are under no obligation to reveal the identity of anyone in the confessional. Canon 979 states that the confessor "is to refrain from asking the name of an accomplice." If a priest asks you for this information, you can refuse to tell him.

- **Is it true that a priest who has been involved with someone sexually cannot give that person absolution for what happened?**

Yes. According to Canon 977 if a priest breaks his vow of celibacy and then absolves his partner for it, that absolution is invalid except in danger of death. Canon 1378 states that a priest will incur automatic excommunication if he gives absolution for a sin against the Sixth Commandment to someone with whom he committed that sin.

- **I haven't been to confession in years, and I don't know what to say or do.**

What happens during confession can vary. Some people still start with the old formula: "Bless me, Father, for I have sinned. It has been 24 years since my last confession."

In other places, you might find that before you can spit out the words, the priest starts the process by introducing himself and reading a passage from Scripture.

Don't worry about doing something wrong. Just tell the priest that it's been a long time since your last confession, and then follow his lead. Most priests realize how uncomfortable you feel. Here are the techniques that five different priests use with fallen away Catholics:

Father John Catoir: I try to make it easy if you have been away from the Church for a long time. I suggest that we run through the Ten Commandments in order to make a general confession for your whole life. All you have to do is say yes or no as I mention each commandment.
When we're through, I ask if there's anything else you want to talk about. I listen, and when you finish talking, I try to put you at ease. I ask you to renew your good intentions and together we thank God for his love and mercy.
Your penance will include all the pain and suffering you've endured over the years since your last confession. I might also ask you to say one Hail Mary and to put a few coins in the poor box in reparation for your sins. St. Peter said that charity overcomes a multitude of sins.
Next, I ask you to make an act of contrition. Some people don't recall the exact formula, but it doesn't matter. You can just tell God you are sorry in your own words. Then I give you absolution and I follow up with this prayer:
"May the passion of Our Lord Jesus Christ, the merits of the Blessed Virgin Mary and all the saints, and what-

ever good you do or suffering you endure, be cause for
the remission of your sins, the increase of grace, and the
gift of everlasting life."

Father Paul Bombadier: The first words out of my mouth are
"Welcome home!" Then I try to engage you in gentle
conversation. If there is some major issue, and often there
is, we talk about that last. First, it is simply welcoming you
back home, and trying to make you feel that God's grace is
the most important and powerful thing that has happened
to you in a long time.
Then we go over the "high points" of the past (or low
points depending on the point of view). If it seems appropriate, I might try to address the issue that kept you away
so long. Most of the time, that issue no longer seems to be
as big a deal as previously thought and some wonderful
healing takes place.
For a penance, I might ask you to say a prayer of thanksgiving to God for bringing you to this moment and to ask
God to help you keep this new commitment to faith. Then
once again, I say, "Welcome back home!"

Father Leon Biernat: When you come in and say that you've
been away for a long time, I suggest that we start with a
prayer of thanksgiving to God that you had the courage
and the strength to come.
The second thing I say is that you don't have to cover
every day of the past 25 years. I suggest that you examine
your conscience in three ways:
• Where are you in your relationship with God? Did you
totally eliminate God from your life? Have you still prayed
on your own? Did you still read the Scriptures?
• Where are you with other people? If you're married, are
you faithful? If you have children, are you responsible in
raising them? If you're working, are you working honestly
— a fair day's work for a day's wage? Do you respect your

neighbor? Are you aware of opportunities when you could
have helped someone but you didn't? Maybe a family is
burned out of their home and you know you can help them
but you choose not to. My favorite is when an elderly
person is going with a walker into the supermarket. Do
you stand and hold the door open, or do you run to beat
them out so they don't slow you down? It's those little
things that happen in all our lives.

• Where are you with yourself? Do you respect your body?
Do you rest? Do you educate yourself? Are you using your
mind? Your talents? Where in your life do you need to
grow? Communication? Patience? Honesty? Ethics?
I ask you to look at the areas where you think you've fallen
a little short. You may look back and see that 25 years ago
something was a real problem but you did improve. I
suggest that we thank God that you have grown.

Father Joe Rogliano: You can always tell when people are
very nervous. They say, "Bless me, Father for I have
sinned. It's been 15 years," and then stop breathing while
they wait for me to yell at them. My typical line is, "Welcome back." I can almost hear the person thinking, "Well,
that wasn't so bad."

Then we talk. Sometimes someone will go on a mile a
minute to get it done. Sometimes people don't know what
to say so I'll help with an examination of conscience.

I don't have you start 20 years back. I have you start last
week. Chances are, if you're in a pattern of sinning, whatever you did last week, you probably did 20 years ago.

Now, there may be something huge and significant that
you've been carrying, and if that's the case, those things
come out at some point and you can unload all of this guilt
that you've carried. I just listen, and then share thoughts.
People usually expect a real pounding penance, but I
always avoid that because I think carrying the guilt of

those sins for so many years has really been penance
enough. If there's something pertinent I will try to match
the penance with the sin. Sometimes I'll give a Scripture
passage to read as a penance. I often assign Psalm 8,
because it talks about our dignity and how great we are in
God's presence.

If you don't remember the act of contrition, I'll pray it with
you. If tears are present, they are tears of cleansing and
part of becoming whole again. If you've wanted that
feeling of being whole again, it is a wonderful experience. I
recently went to confession. I don't think it's easy for a
priest to go, but I think it's important that we go, and I was
so thoroughly cleansed. It makes for a better day, a better
life, a better relationship with everyone and most especially with Our Lord.

Fr. Ron Pecci, OFM: I bring people into the chapel and we sit
down. I usually read one little story from Scripture and
then we just talk. Sometimes people are very focused and
want to talk about a specific situation. They may have
carried this for years and it kept them from the sacraments,
but they never mustered the courage to go to confession.
So I listen. I usually don't have a lot to say in reference to
their sin. They already know the weight of it because they
carried it all those years.

It's so simple, yet people are afraid of letting it go. Some
people are so deeply wounded and they feel so bad about
themselves. They feel separated from God. Some get into a
distorted line of thinking: I can't be good because I'm bad.
The first step to healing is to make the effort. I'll say, "Let it
go. Let yourself be healed. Let yourself be reconciled."
It's a freeing thing. When you are relieved from whatever
darkness you carried, your faith becomes so much more
alive. I usually talk about forgiveness and healing and
going on with life. I give you absolution, we say a prayer of
thanks, and you are on your way.

As you can see, each priest has a different style, but essentially, they all view the sacrament as a form of healing and restoration.

"I found a good and kind priest to hear my confession. I felt as though a great burden had been lifted from my shoulders." M.E., Pennsylvania

"I finally decided to go to confession when my oldest child was receiving his First Penance for I felt it was wrong for me to ask my children to do anything I was unwilling (or afraid) to do. I had been away from the Sacrament of Reconciliation for 15 years and was so nervous. But God was there, leading me to a warm and understanding priest and a whole new life in Jesus." Margaret Sullivan, Massachusetts

"Thanks to an understanding priest, I made my first confession in 17 years and returned to Mass and the Sacraments. I left the Church because of hurt feelings. I now see the need to forgive the priest who hurt me and to move on. I was so afraid that the Church would not take me back. I was absolutely numb when I walked up to the rectory for my appointment. But the priest I saw was so kind and understanding. I am assured beyond any doubt that coming back was the right thing. To anyone who is wondering if they can/should return, I say, 'Yes!'" H.C., San Francisco, California

Chapter Notes

"a grave violation of God's law...": CCC, # 1855.
"does not deprive the sinner of sanctifying grace...": CCC, # 1863.

CHAPTER 20

Why People Come Home

"I returned after the death of my mother. We had a Catholic burial for her and it was at that time that I decided to seek re-entry." *Gene Kinnaly, Jacksonville, Florida*

"For years, I experimented with Methodist, Baptist, Pentecostal, Vineyard and non-denominational fellowships, but something was missing. I felt for the longest time a tugging on my heart, a call back to the Catholic Church. My born-again friends think I'm crazy. They keep telling me I'll lose my salvation, but I can't get that feeling of 'Home' out of my system. It feels right when I walk through the door." *Stephanie Roy*

"I would prefer to think of myself as a 'wayward' Catholic rather than alienated. I really can't put a finger on the exact reason for my renewed devotion, but it is safe to say that having children of my own has been an important factor." *D.M.G., Pennsylvania*

"My path back to the Church was through Transcendental Meditation, the Unitarian Church, art, music, having a baby and getting a divorce. Oh my!" *Tracy Bier, Seattle, Washington*

At age 22, Jean Fox left the Church. At the time, she was

living in New York's Greenwich Village, where she worked as a visiting nurse. She considered herself an agnostic.

While making calls one afternoon, a storm forced her to seek shelter in a public library. "I put my hand on the stacks and pulled out a book called *Our Lady of Fatima* by William Thomas Walsh," she recalls. "My mind was saying, 'Who could ever believe this trash in the 20th century?' But I cracked the book and my heart started to burn."

The next day, Jean found herself back at the library. She opened the book again and the same burning sensation seized her. "That was the beginning. It was like Our Lady got hold of me in a mysterious way."

Several months later, Jean was walking down Broadway, thinking about who would be considered the most important figure since the beginning of history. Like a flash of lightning she knew the answer was Jesus Christ. "It was a deep, infused knowledge that was so radical everything in me was instant revolution," she insists. "I went to confession that Saturday, and said, 'Father, please, I just need forgiveness through you for turning my back against God and the Church.'"

Today, Jean Fox lives in Combermere, Ontario where she is the director of women at Madonna House, a Catholic community of men, women and priests who dedicate their lives to serving the poor. Within the course of each year, Jean meets people from all over the world, who left the Church and struggle to find their way back. She understands what they are going through, and she assures them that it is God who is drawing them back.

While God is at the center of each person's decision to return to the Church, the circumstances surrounding people's return are as varied as the reasons why they left. In his study for the United States Catholic Conference, Dean R. Hoge grouped people who return into four broad categories:

1. **Marriage-Life Returnees**. These people are strongly in-

fluenced by a spouse or concern for their marriages. About one-fourth also report some spiritual motivation.

"My wife and I were both fallen-away Catholics. When she decided that she wanted to go back to the Church, it became a real bone of contention. I really thought it would split us apart. One night, after arguing about the situation, I got hit by God's cosmic baseball bat and realized that I was supposed to stop the nonsense and be Catholic again." *J.L.*

2. **Family-Life Returnees.** Their motivation stems from concern for their children's religious upbringing and a desire for family religious solidarity. About one-third also report spiritual motivations.

"I'll be 39 this year, and haven't been in a Catholic church since I was 12. Last week, I went to the Catholic elementary school to discuss the possibility of sending my son there. I saw the old familiar pictures of the Virgin Mary and a cross with Jesus Christ hanging on it. I watched an elderly woman enter the church and genuflect. It was just an unbelievable whack on the side of the head sort of experience. Why hadn't I come back before??? My husband was baptized as an infant in the Catholic Church, but that's as far as religion went in his family. We have a long way to go, but I think we're heading in the right direction." *Janice Haber, Guthrie, Oklahoma*

3. **Guilt-Feeling Returnees.** These people feel guilty about leaving the Church. They sometimes feel nostalgic about their religious upbringing, and they long for the good things they remember about growing up Catholic.

"When I was growing up in New England everyone went to church. Our parish had carnivals every year. Our neighborhoods were built around our parishes. I left the

Church because I had views I felt were not Catholic. Now I am willing to rethink my views because I feel the need to raise my children in a Catholic community. The Catholic Church can offer the support and the programs from CCD to scouts to pot luck dinners. I have many things to be thankful for — a good life, a great husband, healthy children. I'm coming home because I'm thankful for my life." *Sharyn Bush, Florida*

4. **Seeker Returnees**. These people search for an answer to a spiritual need or a sense of purpose in their lives.

"I got a sheet of paper out and divided it into two columns. In the first I put all the reasons I could think of for why I should return. In the other I wrote why I left and should not return. It took several tries, but finally I saw that I simply missed God." *Carol Samuelson, Jamestown, New York*

While most people do not mention spiritual motivation as the primary reason for coming back, in 41% of all cases they mention it in conjunction with some other influence.

"Something was always calling me back, and I always felt such peace when I did go to Mass. I soon found a longing to go to Mass daily, but I really couldn't figure out why. I began to go (causing many raised eyebrows among family and friends) and I began a journey that has been a lot like a roller-coaster ride." *Margaret Sullivan, Massachusetts*

"I missed the Sacraments, especially the Eucharist. Now I have been to confession and am becoming more active in the Parish." *M.G., Pennsylvania*

In almost half of the cases, people admitted that another person — sometimes a spouse, a child, friends or family — played a major role in their decision to return.

"I met and married a nice Catholic girl. She became the evidence of God in my life. It took several years of marriage, but after time what become most clear was God was pouring out his love of me through her. She was not pushy. She simply loved me. As time passed and our relationship deepened, I gradually was open to the moving of the Spirit in me." *Joe Hattick, Colorado Springs, Colorado*

"My return to the Church about 5 years ago was related to my oldest son and his question to me at Christmas about who Jesus was. I was not satisfied with my own answer, and so the quest began." *M. Loebig, Pittsburgh, Pennsylvania*

"A year and a half ago, my mother passed away. A short time later, I lost my job and all the money I had put down on a deposit for a house. A friend challenged me to go to church for four straight Sundays without any excuses. I was feeling down at the time, so I thought it couldn't hurt. Well, the first time I went, I didn't feel a whole lot different, but as the weeks went on I began to feel good again. It almost felt good to be back to the Church." *Joe MacKay, Seattle, Washington*

Thirteen percent of Catholics who return to the Church attend other churches during the time they are away.

"I guess it really comes down to the fact that I was searching and at the time did not find what I was looking for in the Catholic Church. After some initial breaking away I started hearing how awful the Catholic Church was, and I have to say, some of it I agreed with. I started making my rounds of churches that I thought might be more on target with my personal beliefs. I was trying to find someplace I felt comfortable. For a while that was the Vineyard Christian Fellowship, but then I started feeling uncomfortable, and was leaving church feeling very empty. Gradu-

ally I worked my way back to the Catholic Church."
Stephanie Roy

Some people fall away from the Church several times during their lives. For example, some become active or inactive with job transfers to different cities. Others leave as young adults, but return when they have children. Some leave again when their children grow up, but return when they begin to face their own mortality.

"I was born Catholic and left twice. I came back when I began to see that the Roman Catholic Church is the most fundamental expression of Christianity as well as the most diverse. Receiving Jesus in the flesh is a thrill NOTHING can match. Most people know in their hearts that there is truth here, and that's why they keep circling around. That's why the thirst may fade, but it never goes away completely." *B.W.*

Twenty-five percent mentioned personal problems, illness, divorce, the death of a loved one or some other life-shaking experience as factors influencing their return.

"After a medical crisis with my husband, God answered my prayer. I went to church that Sunday and the parish was beginning a Lenten mission by the Redemptorist Fathers. I went to the mission and the message to return was strong, especially the message that any sin and all sins are forgiven if repentance is sincere. I have since returned to the faith, and I couldn't be happier." *V.F.*

Some people mention something specific — such as Marriage Encounter, or Cursillo, or a charismatic prayer group — as influencing their decision to return. Others credit a book they read or a religious program on radio or television.
For Frank Barbarossa of Amherst, New York, it was a Prot-

estant radio program that led him to a deeper relationship with
God and the Catholic Church:

> I was in San Francisco for a medical conference and
> came back to my hotel room around 10 p.m. All of a
> sudden the clock radio came on. It was a Protestant
> preacher. I listened for five or ten minutes before I finally
> figured out how to turn it off. The next night, I must
> have dozed off while I was reading, and the radio came
> on again. This time it was a different preacher.
> About a month later, I was fiddling with the radio on
> my way into work and I found one of the programs I
> had heard in San Francisco. After that, I started listen-
> ing to Christian radio broadcasts in the car and reading
> Scripture. It changed my life. I didn't know there was
> such a thing as a relationship with God. I never got that
> message from the Catholic Church. Now I believe it was
> God calling me to a deeper level of faith, and I'm a bet-
> ter Catholic because of it. It's not like I was this way one
> day and the next day I was different. It was like a seed
> that had to develop.

For many people, like Frank Barbarossa, the process of
coming back to the Church involves a spiritual conversion,
which changes them in some way. Over half of the people who
return to the Church say their family life has changed. Seventy-
three percent now attend Mass weekly. Seventy percent say
religion has become important in their lives. Sixty-eight percent
find their outlook toward life changed. Forty percent notice
changes in their personal routines that include spending more
time going to church or participating in parish activities. Nearly
one-fourth have made new friends. Thirteen percent stopped
smoking, drinking or using drugs.

"I'm always surprised at how many people from the Come
Home program call me years later to let me know how things
worked out for them," says Father Ron Pecci, OFM. "I met one
man in a lumber yard, who told me that coming back to the

Church changed his marriage and his children. Now they worship together and get involved in the parish. Another man told me that he switched jobs because he could no longer work in a place where he had to manipulate and exploit people."

It is estimated that more than half of the people who stop going to Mass eventually come back to the Church. The question that many people ask at Come Home programs is: What do they come back to?

Chapter Notes

In a 1981 study for the United States Catholic Conference...: and ff. Hoge, pp. 138-139.

CHAPTER 21

What Do They Come Back To?

"What thrills me is the acceptance I've felt by others in our parish. Whenever I'm at a loss to figure out what's going on, I just explain that I haven't been to church since I was a pre-teen (I'm 38 now), and people actually smile and are so generous with their explanations and help. These are total strangers, and yet they're glad I've returned. That speaks volumes, doesn't it?" *Janice Haber, Guthrie, Oklahoma*

"I've come to learn through my experience that it isn't what the Church gives us, it's what we give of ourselves. After all, the Church is not the building that we go to or the priest that says Mass. We, the people, are the Church." *Stephanie Roy*

"If there's one thing I'm getting from conversations I've had with practicing Catholics, it's that they also end up not agreeing with everything but just sort of plunge on ahead. I can live with that." *M.R.G., Chicago, Illinois*

Sometimes it seems as if everyone in the Catholic Church is taking a stand about something: The Church is too liberal. The Church is too conservative. There aren't enough priests. We should have married priests. What about women priests? The Pope says no women priests. I disagree with the Pope. You're not allowed to disagree with the Pope. There's not enough inclusive language. There's too much inclusive language. The reforms of Vatican II have gone too far. The reforms have not gone far enough. The Bishops should take a stronger stand on current events and issues. The Bishops should mind their own business. The Church is anti-intellectual. The Church is too intellectual. Theologians should be silenced. Theologians play an important role in the Church. The Church is a mess. The Church is stronger than it has ever been. Blame it on the curia. What is the curia?

People who are in the process of returning to the Catholic Church will find all of this and more. You'll find caring priests and cranky priests. You'll find people who are kind, understanding and non-judgmental. You find people caught up in power plays, gossip, bickering, and self-serving little cliques. You'll meet people who want to bring new ideas into the parish, and people who want everything to stay just the way it's always been.

Why would someone want to come home to what seems like a Church filled with chaos?

"I think there's a lot of beauty in the Catholic Church," suggests Msgr. William Stanton. "I am ordained 47 years, and there have been some very tough times, but I've never regretted being a Catholic. I've enjoyed my life as a priest helping people, suffering with people, rejoicing with them. There is a family atmosphere in the Catholic Church. There is grace abounding. There is a lot of love if you just know where to tap in."

Most people who return to the Church find out rather quickly that different parishes have different personalities. An important part of finding the love in the Church that Msgr. Stanton mentions involves finding a parish where you feel comfortable. Some parishes have traditional liturgies. Others have great homilies. Some focus on social justice issues. Others feature special devotions. Some have music that sounds like choirs of angels, while others have people singing, clapping and waving their arms. Some parishes will seem open, welcoming and accommodating, while others have lots of rules and requirements. In a five-page letter, Bishop John McCarthy of Austin, Texas warned parishes in his diocese against insensitivity to people's needs. He pointed out that when parishes set down "unconditional and legalistic demands," it's no surprise that people refuse to jump through the hoops. He asked why parishes sometimes treat "nominal" Catholics, who come back to the parish in need of sacraments for themselves or their children as if they were "not worthy" because they didn't comply with the parish "requirements." He concluded with the challenge that pastors use a little "horse sense."

There are over 19,000 parishes in the United States, and more than 95% of Americans live within a thirty-minute drive of a Catholic parish. If you encounter a parish with unbendable rules where you are treated as a "problem" or made to feel as if you are somehow "unworthy," maybe you should use a little "horse sense" and find another parish.

> "I went to three different parishes, and I found weary people listening to readers and priests with near-hypnotic voices. At the fourth parish, I found some life, some excitement to the Mass." *D.G.*

> "I found a parish in our diocese that offers a traditional Latin Mass with Gregorian Chant and incense. I finally feel as if I have come home." *C.C.*

> "I found a parish where they changed all the hymns and Scripture readings to eliminate any gender reference." *G.R.*

> "I went to a suburban parish and felt boxed-in. So I went into the city and found a Franciscan parish where they

work with the homeless, the poor, and all kinds of people who are on the edge. I think Jesus worked with people on the edge, and that's what I want to do, too." *E.Q.*

What should you look for when shopping for a parish? The answer to that question depends on your own personal preferences and preferred style of worship. Surveys of returning Catholics reveal the qualities most people would most like to see in a parish include:

• Personal and more accessible priests in a warm and personal parish.

"I attend a church 20 minutes from my home and it is well worth the trip. The parish feels like an extended family where parishioners truly treat the parish as their own. They are very welcoming to new members." *Margaret Sullivan, Massachusetts*

• More support for family living — religious education, adult education, and family oriented programs.

"I'd like to see more Bible study in Catholic churches. It's really difficult if you try to do it yourself — especially if you haven't had any experience reading Scripture." *Frank Barbarossa, Amherst, New York*

• More help for divorced people and for couples who desire to return to the Church after remarriage.

"Many people, like myself, who were away from the Church because of divorce are afraid they will not be accepted. I am now a member of the Beginning Experience team in my diocese. The vision of Beginning Experience is to help people to be healed, transformed, and free to love again." *Lenne Shields-Orona, Des Moines, Iowa*

"Parish membership means commitment and that's always a two-way street," says Father Robert Zapfel. "If you're going to shop, don't just look for how your needs can be met, look also to where your gifts and talents can be used, and where you can become an active member."

"I was away from the Church for many years. When I returned I decided to share my concerns with the pastor about how new people were treated. New parishioners and 'returnees' now receive a Welcome Packet containing a brochure that lists all the parish organizations, contact names, Mass and confession schedules, names of parish priests and their specific ministries." *P.L., Virginia*

It's good to keep in mind that no matter where you go, there will be things about the parish, the priests, and the people that you may not like. That's human nature. Sometimes you have to weigh the good against the bad. Sometimes you have to look at everything from a different angle. It helps if you can be open to changes that may have taken place while you were away. If something seems strange, ask about it. There may be a very good reason.

"I returned to the Church after a 10-year absence. It used to be that after the priest left the altar, it was a mad dash to the parking lot, but I was surprised to find people kneeling for a brief period before heading out the door. I found out later that it was a parish custom to stay and say a Hail Mary or a prayer for your family after Mass." *Patricia Embury, Rochester, New York*

In some cases, you may have to simply overlook some of the minor irritations and focus on factors that are more positive.

"I used to be frustrated by bad homilies and unfriendly congregations, but recently my heart has been changed.

Now the Mass is an intensely spiritual and renewing experience for me because my focus is on Jesus Christ. He is there in the readings and in the songs no matter how badly they are read or sung." *G.W.*

A hunger for the Eucharist is a common thread that runs through the stories of Catholics who have come home.

"In no other place will you find the very real presence of Jesus in the Eucharist. I am sustained in a way I cannot explain by attending Mass and receiving the Eucharist." *Margaret Sullivan, Massachusetts*

The bottom line for most returning Catholics means putting God first and letting everything else fall into place.

"Stop thinking about returning to a Church and start thinking about returning to a relationship with Jesus Christ. Jesus is faithfully and expectantly awaiting your return. He loves you and he has already forgiven and forgotten every sin you ever committed. So, why don't you take his lead and forgive yourself? When you and Jesus are reconciled, your relationship with the Church will be clear to you." *Frank Johnston, Cumming, Georgia*

Chapter Notes

In a five-page letter, Bishop John McCarthy of Austin, Texas…: Ginny Cunningham, "Sensitivity Keeps Catholics in the Fold," *US Catholic*, March, 1996, p. 27.

There are over 19,000 parishes…: Hoge, p. 181.

CHAPTER 22

Coming Back to the Catholic Church

"I started my journey back to the Catholic Church via a 'sack lunch' program that a local parish sponsored. They make lunches for the homeless. It was a safe way for me to get involved in the Church indirectly, yet have a chance to view and get a feel for how the Church is today. I was pleased to see a Church that was alive. I was looking for something different than what I had grown up with, and there it was." *H.M.T., Seattle, Washington*

"I started by going back to Mass every Sunday and then continued in a weekly class for persons wanting to return to the Church. Our parish has been supportive and wonderful. In January 1996, my children were baptized. I feel as though we are home." *R.G.*

"If I had to look around for an appropriate program, I would look for one that requires open bibles, open minds, open eyes, and open ears. RCIA worked for me because I didn't have to be embarrassed by my ignorance." *Frank Johnston, Cumming, Georgia*

In the fall of 1996, radio stations in Buffalo, New York broadcast 30-second messages from Bishop Henry Mansell inviting Catholics, who felt separated from the Church because of marriage problems, doubts, painful memories or other personal reasons, to a Come Home lecture series. "I promise you no pressure. No strings attached," Bishop Mansell said. "And please be assured that my prayers are always with you."

The unique part of this monthly lecture series is that fallen-away Catholics designed it. The people in this little group had vastly different reasons for being away from the Church, but they brainstormed ideas and selected the topics they felt would interest other alienated Catholics. Several parishes agreed to sponsor the events, and the Bishop agreed to extend the invitation. None of this would have happened if this small group of fallen-away Catholics had not taken the initiative to do something.

Increasingly, parishes and dioceses are starting outreach programs for alienated Catholics, but there is no uniformity nationwide. In some parts of the country, parishes have designed their own programs to bring people back. At a parish in Wynnwood, Pennsylvania, for example, the pastor printed Christmas cards with a note asking people who only come to church occasionally to respond anonymously as to what keeps them away. At the bottom of the card, he added, "Would you like to talk about it? If so, leave your name and number, and I'll give you a call."

Some parishes filter fallen-away Catholics through the Rite of Christian Initiation for Adults (RCIA), which is the process by which converts are brought into the Church. If you never made your First Communion or never received the Sacrament of Confirmation, RCIA might be a good option for you. If you have school-age children, who need to receive the sacraments, you will find that many parishes use a modified RCIA program for children.

Carrie Kemp and Father Don Pologruto, CSP developed a "Come Home" model in the mid-1980's that has been adopted in many parts of the country for inviting lapsed Catholics to a series of information sessions. Father William McKee, CSSR developed a program that begins with a guest speaker at Sunday Masses, who urges parishioners to invite friends and neighbors to a series of special sessions for inactive Catholics. Father John Forliti of St. Paul, Minnesota started Alienated Catholics Anonymous, a 12-step program where people meet in small groups and help each other on their journey back to the Church. Father Joseph Breighner of Baltimore designed a four day parish mission for returning Catholics. Father Michael Everden, CSP developed a small group program for returning Catholics. The Paulists offer a direct mail program called "Another Look," but the term "Another Look" is also used in some places to describe a series of information sessions.

"I make the distinction between the evangelization models of these programs and the sacramental models," says Father Robert Kennedy of the St. Bernard Institute in Rochester, New York.

Father Kennedy would group information sessions such as Another Look and Come Home into the first category because they are designed to identify needs, answer questions, and then allow the participants to return to the Church on their own. Some people like the anonymity of this approach. Others like the fact that the sessions were non-judgmental and information-oriented with no commitment required.

- "It provided the opportunity to return to the Church with no questions asked."

- "It began to answer some of my questions, which is what I had hoped."

- "I liked the informality. No sign-ins. No solicitations."

Most programs like Come Home run for a limited time period, such as 3 to 6 sessions, but in some places, faith sharing groups have formed for people who want to continue with a weekly or monthly discussion. The emphasis, however, is based on information and discussion, with no organized sacramental component.

"That is not to say that they exclude the sacraments," Father Kennedy explains, "but the emphasis is on reacquainting people with the Church."

According to Father Kennedy's classifications, Re-Membering and Landings would qualify as sacramental models.

Re-Membering was started by Father James Lopresti, and is modeled partly on RCIA, and partly on the ancient Order of Penitents, which was the process by which the early Christians received people back into the Church. Throughout the year, Re-Membering groups meet for discussion, presentations, and prayer — sometimes weekly, sometimes once or twice a month, sometimes for a block of time at various intervals. Each person in a Re-Membering group is assigned a sponsor or companion. The goal is to help a person work through the reasons for their alienation from the Church and lead them to healing, conversion, and an adult faith commitment. On Ash Wednesday, the participants are initiated into the Order of Penitents, when they receive ashes at one of the parish Masses.

> "During Lent, they spend time in prayer and meditation, with Sunday and daily Scriptures, in conversations with their companion. They will probably seek the wisdom of a spiritual guide and confessor. Their penitential journey is incorporated into the prayer of the whole Church community. They celebrate a process of sacramental penance and reconciliation beginning with the confession of God's mercy on Ash Wednesday and culminating with public absolution on Holy Thursday. And finally, they joyfully celebrate their return to the Eucharistic table with the parish community on Holy Thursday."

Landings is a Paulist program that involves 8 to 10 weeks of small group faith sharing, prayer and discussion with people from the parish serving as facilitators and sponsors. The Landings coordinators believe it is important to protect the privacy of people in the process of returning so they avoid any public presentation of the groups at parish Masses or penance services. Instead, participants make a private retreat with the others members of their small group where they receive Communion together for the first time. "Near the end of the Mass, the leader of the group will give each person a little token to show that they're not just formally connected to the sacraments and to Rome, but they have also been loved back by these people of this parish," explains Landings founder Father Jac Campbell, CSP.

Mariann Ferretti, who was away from the Church for 25 years, is now a Landings facilitator in San Francisco. "Most of the Landings groups go on and meet periodically on their own as a small faith sharing group. A lot of the people who come through Landings get very involved in the parish. It's a wonderful experience for most people, but it's not for everybody."

Different people have different needs. For some, an information-based program might not be enough; for others a weekly faith sharing group might be too much. Some people may need specialized help for problems involving annulments, bereavement, or abuse. Others may need a one-on-one session with a priest.

Father Campbell insists that no one should ever feel pressured or obligated to come back to the Church through Landings or any other program. There is no right or wrong way to come back to the Church. Canon law requires only confession and a return to Mass and Communion. If that's all you want or need, you should be able to find a sympathetic priest in a parish, in a local retreat center, at a Catholic college or in a Catholic hospital. Don't give up if you can't connect with someone on your first or second try. Somewhere, there is a priest waiting for your call.

Msgr. William Gallagher insists that the Church is like a family, and it's important for you to feel as if you're part of a family:

The family needs you. You are a facet in the diamond that is the Church. Without you, we are still incomplete. We want you to belong. We want you to recognize that as a member of this family you will have access to so many things that you might not have access to if you were out there alone. The Catholic Church gives you a prayer life to support the good days and the bad days. It gives you the company of other fellow travelers. It exposes you to wisdom that is thousands of years old. It puts you in touch with all of the presences of Christ that we claim exist: in Scripture, in prayer, in the company of others, in the Bread of Life in the Eucharist.

But when you come back, you should do it like you would if you were going back to your parents to settle differences. We can't fix everything. But we should face the fact that if we are at odds; we should settle it. We may never agree totally, but we can settle it, for the good of everyone.

If you're not ready to talk to a priest, try going to Mass. It doesn't have to be on a Sunday when the church is bursting with people. You can slip into a weekday Mass in the morning or on your lunch hour without ever being noticed.

"I began to feel a strange longing to go back to the Church. The first time I went I realized that I was the one who had cut myself off from God. The truth hit me with a force that was almost physical, but at the same time, God was there comforting and consoling me. I don't know if this makes sense, but it was an overwhelming experience of love and forgiveness." E.G.

No matter what anyone else tells you, the spiritual longing you feel is God trying to draw you back to himself.

"I remember when I had my first tangible experience of God. It happened one Sunday, when we reached the part in the Mass where we say, 'Lord, I am not worthy to receive you, but only say the word and I shall be healed.' God decided to let me know what His healing would feel like. I hadn't been receiving the Eucharist, by my choice at this point. But now, I wanted to receive it. I wanted to know that feeling again and again." *Frank Johnston, Cumming, Georgia*

Coming back to the Church is not an event as much as it is a process. It starts when you open yourself to the movement of God in your life, but the decision whether or not to move in that direction is entirely up to you. Some people will return to the Church. Others will choose to stay away. Some will remain undecided.

What about you? Could you ever come back to the Catholic Church?

Chapter Notes

"During Lent, they spend time in prayer and meditation...": Sarah Harmony, *Re-Membering: The Ministry of Welcoming Alienated and Inactive Catholics*, Collegeville, Minnesota: The Liturgical Press, 1991, p. 18.

Afterword

One of the delightful features of going around the Diocese to celebrate Mass and visit the parishioners is meeting people after Mass who in recent years have become Catholics or have come back to the Church after a long time away. The radiant smiles say it all, but nevertheless I sometimes ask them, "Are you happy you did it?"

When they get over the shock that I would ask such an inane question and they utter a prayer, silently, that the bishop will soon wake up and smell the coffee, their answers are revealing:

> "I feel more complete."
> "The situation at home is so much better."
> "I'm a happier person."
> "There's more meaning to my life."
> "My life is more structured."
> "I've got better perspective."
> "I'm more responsible."
> "I love coming to Church."
> "I work better."
> "I get along better with people."
> "I'm doing things that are worthwhile."
> "I'm praying better."
> "There's a joy in my life I did not know before."

Those reflections just reinforce for me the value of Lorie Duquin's work.

If you are one of those people who jump to the last pages

before reading a book, let me tell you, you are in for a treat. The book is a spiritual experience, or rather a series of spiritual experiences. Lorie Duquin, in her person and in her writing, is as positive and affirming as anyone can be this side of the Eternal Banquet. She goes all the way with realism and arrives at a point beyond. Her sprightly writing style reveals a friendliness that runs like a golden thread through the entire work. She opens up serious issues, and the sensitive concern with which she describes situations shows her to be a true friend. Her love for the Church is contagious.

If you have read all the book up to this, I give you permission to skip the Afterword and still be able to say you read the entire work. What you know now, though, is that Lorie Duquin is not only a thinker and a writer, she is a doer.

I was Bishop of Buffalo for only a short time when she and other former fallen-away Catholics visited me and told me they were trying to put together a lecture series on topics that touched questions and concerns of fallen-away Catholics about the Church.

My first reaction was, "Thank God for you. Your experiences and development should provide effective help for others." When they asked if I would personally and publicly invite people who felt separated from the Church to attend these sessions, I agreed because the program seemed to reach for people where they were and to do so with warmth and understanding.

During the course of the lecture series, I saw with new insight some of the pain people experienced when they were away from the Church and how much they wanted to return. Some of the letters I received reflected a deep inner struggle:

Dear Bishop Mansell:

Thank you for the Come Home program. I hope that this will have a healing effect on me and help me spiritually. This has been wonderful.

* * *

Dear Bishop:

We enjoyed the first lecture on Come Home. Our concerns center around divorce and annulment. We have many questions about the process. We all thank you for giving us an opportunity to come here tonight. We all feel that our roots are in the Catholic Church and we'd like to come home.

* * *

Dear Bishop Mansell:

We thank you for encouraging people to Come Home! Father Joe, this evening, reached out to us and invited us to Come Home. He expressed a concern for the concerns of the people in attendance. He addressed the issue of reaching out to people, particularly those who have been hurt or think that they have been hurt by the Church. This series is a wonderful idea and the very fact that it was so well attended, there must be a need for this type of program.

* * *

Dear Bishop:

I am attending the Come Home program with the hope of being found when I was lost. A sinner I am in many ways, but I have a strong feeling of love for God, but have had a hard time showing it. I know I probably will not get to talk to you about my problems, so I think that you have these people along with some of your priests to help me solve my problems. I will try this because somewhere and sometime I hope the answer will come my way.

* * *

Dear Bishop Mansell,

I have many questions and doubts that stem from years of memorizing but never knowing and understanding aspects of the Catholic religion. The 60's and 70's were filled with these doubts for me, and I'm not even certain I want the answers yet. But I'll take it a day at a time, one step at a time. We'll see...

* * *

Dear Bishop,

We feel it is a well-needed program for all Catholics who have left the Church. We need to know God has not turned His back on us, for whatever reason we decided to stay away. We need to know that there are people out there who care and are willing to help us through our pain.

* * *

Dear Bishop,

We feel the Come Home Lecture Series is very worthwhile. It is good to know the Church is concerned and is taking steps to reconcile. Many of us are anxious to come home. You would be amazed to see the number of people here, people who have taken that giant first step.

* * *

Too many people have been hurt by someone or something in the Church. If this kind of pain is part of your story, I would like to apologize on behalf of the Church for the ways in which you have been hurt. I know a simple apology does not seem like much, but it is a first step, and I am sincere in the hope that it will begin to heal some of your pain and bring you closer to God's infinite love.

God's love is the beginning. God always loves us first. Our lives are a response. If at this point you are pondering the question which forms the title of this book, please know that you are not alone. We are here to help.

The English essayist, Malcolm Muggeridge, described his experience of becoming a Catholic: "In the end it was a sense of homecoming, of picking up the pieces of a life that had been missing, of responding to a bell that had long been ringing, of finding a place at a table that had long been left vacant."

The place at the table is waiting...

Henry J. Mansell, D.D.
Bishop of Buffalo

Come Home

Father Flavian Walsh, OFM   or   St. Francis Church
Our Lady of Holy Angels   135 West 31st Street
473 Main Street   New York, NY 10001-3439
Little Falls, NJ 07424-1132   212-735-8500
201-256-5200
fax 201-256-0185

Come Home Lecture Series

Diocese of Buffalo
Communications Department
Catholic Center
795 Main Street
Buffalo, NY 14203
716-847-8719

Landings

Fr. Jac Campbell, CSP   or   Joan A. Horn
Landings National Director   Landings National Coordinator
5 Park Street   3311 Big Bend
Boston, MA 02108   Austin, TX 78731
617-720-5986   512-452-7566
e-mail JACSP@aol.com   e-mail horn@mail.utexas.edu

Madonna House

Combermere, Ontario
Canada K0J 1L0
613-756-3713

National Association of Catholic Diocesan Lesbian and Gay Ministries

Father Jim Schexnayder
NACSLGM
433 Jefferson Street
Oakland, CA 94607
510-465-9344
e-mail NACDLGM @aol.com

Paulist National Catholic Evangelization Association
3031 4th Street, N.E.
Washington, DC 20017
202-832-5022

Re-Membering
The North American Forum on the Catechumenate
7715 Leesburg Pike, Suite 308
Falls Church, VA 22043-2301
703-534-8082
Fax: 703-534-8086

The Redemptorists
Liguori Mission House
10 Liguori Drive
Liguori, MO 63057-9999
314-464-6999

The Beginning Experience
(a peer ministry for separated, divorced & widowed persons)
1209 Washington Blvd.
Detroit, MI 48226
313-965-5110
Fax 313-965-5557

St. Jude Media Ministry
Father John Catoir
P.O. Box 17
Clifton, NJ 07011